READER'S GUIDE TO THE GOSPELS

THE MODERN READER'S GUIDE TO THE GOSPELS

by William Hamilton

ASSOCIATION PRESS · NEW YORK

First printing 1960 in one
volume under the title
THE MODERN READER'S GUIDE TO THE GOSPELS

Issued earlier as three separate Reflection Books: *The Modern Reader's Guide to Matthew and Luke* © 1959 by National Board of Young Men's Christian Associations; *The Modern Reader's Guide to Mark* © 1959 by National Board of Young Men's Christian Associations; *The Modern Reader's Guide to John* © 1959 by National Board of Young Men's Christian Associations.

Association Press, 291 Broadway, New York 7, N. Y.

Library of Congress catalog card number: 60-6562

 I

Printed in the United States of America

Preface

The purpose of this "Modern Reader's Guide to the Gospels" is simple: to enable the reader to understand intelligently four basic Christian documents. I am convinced that lay groups in the churches and students on the campuses are beginning to realize that careful Bible study is one form of Christian obedience that must not be avoided. This guide is meant to be a contribution to that study, without which Protestantism, cannot effectively live, think, or act.

By itself, this volume would be useless and unintelligible. The reader will need copies of the Gospels according to Matthew, Mark, Luke, and John. These can be found in most homes and bookstores. Even more helpful would be a copy of *Gospel Parallels,* published by Thomas Nelson & Sons. Part One, combining the gospels of Matthew and Luke, has a slightly different form and function from Parts Two and Three, dealing with Mark and with John, because the writers of Matthew and Luke have a single purpose. Full coverage of all the material in these two gospels could not be achieved, but the major sections are dealt with, the material is arranged in a roughly chronological way, and the reader will be able to discover what the authors of these gospels were attempting to do as they presented their witness.

There are many useful and even sprightly books *about* the Bible on the market today. Their function is in general to make us feel that we ought to read the Bible and that we might find it enjoyable. The Bible, however, still presents some problems to the modern reader as he faces the actual text, and so this book tries to meet some of those problems for the person—alone or in a group—who is willing to sit before the material and allow it to speak to him.

There is little that is original in the content of this guide. I have drawn heavily on the work of experts in the field of biblical studies: William Manson, G. E. P. Cox, Sherman Johnson, S. MacLean Gilmour and some others, in the guide to Matthew and Luke; Frederick C. Grant, A. M. Hunter, C. H. Dodd, Vincent Taylor, and some others, in the guide to Mark; and W. F. Howard, C. K. Barrett, William Temple, Sir Edwyn Hoskyns, and some others, in the guide to John. In one sense, the work of the author has been little more than that of an editor, but the form may be slightly more original. This is neither a study guide such as the student movement sometimes uses nor a commentary such as scholars hope that Christian ministers use. It is something in between—fuller and more technical than the first, less technical and more practical than the second—and therefore of more value, I hope, for the layman.

For those who prefer it, this one volume guide to the gospels is also available as three separate, soft-covered Reflection Books: *The Modern Reader's Guide to Matthew and Luke, The Modern Reader's Guide to Mark,* and *The Modern Reader's Guide to John.*

The citations and references to the Bible herein are from the Revised Standard Version of The Holy Bible.

WILLIAM HAMILTON

Contents

PART TWO : MARK

PART THREE : JOHN

PART ONE

MATTHEW AND LUKE

Introduction

Matthew and Luke are treated together as a single story. In so doing, some sacrifice of completeness has been made, but by this means the reader will be able to understand that both these writers have a single purpose: to declare the meaning and content of the ministry, death, and resurrection of Jesus Christ. This section includes a number of references to Mark's gospel, and though it is not necessary that a study of Mark be made prior to this study, the reader may want at another time to look carefully at Mark, for both Matthew and Luke depend heavily on it.

Mark was the earliest gospel; it appeared sometime between A.D. 65 and 70. Shortly after, two new gospels appeared: Luke, probably written for the church in Rome in the 80's or 90's; and Matthew, written in Syria, perhaps Antioch, between 90 and 100.

As you go through Matthew and Luke, you can see that they both make ample use of Mark. Long passages are taken over almost verbatim, others are used only slightly revised, and Mark's order is usually followed. Matthew and Luke, however, have access to a collection of Jesus' teachings not found in Mark. This collection is called the "Q" source. And, in addition, Matthew and Luke each has a body of material which the author of the gospel has collected himself, used only by him, called respectively "M" and "L" by scholars. If you imagine Matthew or Luke sitting down to compile his gospel, he will have Mark before him; he will be using a document or collection of early church notes on Jesus' teaching; and he will have his own independently collected source.

Luke's gospel is the first volume of a two-volume work (Acts being the second) addressed to a certain Roman official named Theophilus (Luke 1:3). He may have been a pagan interested in Christianity for its own sake; or he may have been an official involved in the persecutions of the Christians. We can be fairly certain that the author was the Luke mentioned by Paul as a physician and as one of his early associates (Colossians 4:14, Philemon 24).

There are some special characteristics that distinguish Luke. He is anxious to prove that Christianity is not dangerous to the state, and he shows this by proving that Christianity is the true successor to the synagogue, deserving of the protection that the Romans offered to Judaism. Luke stresses the universal claims of Christianity, its absence of racial limitations. In the life of Jesus, he underlines a number of things that Mark merely notes: the importance of prayer in Jesus' life; the proper use of wealth; sympathy for the poor. Luke, like Matthew, takes Mark as a basis. He adds extra material on Jesus' birth and resurrection, and he includes far more material on Jesus' teaching ministry. He is the most skillful writer among the authors of the synoptics, and the most responsible historian of the three.

It is generally agreed that the author of the Gospel according to Matthew is not the Matthew who was the disciple of Jesus. It would be hard to understand why a disciple and an eyewitness would be so dependent on Mark, who was not an eyewitness.

The one fact that is important to notice about Matthew's gospel is its strong emphasis on Christianity as a new law. Matthew seems directed to Jews or to recently converted ex-Jews, showing them that Christianity is the true fulfillment of the Jewish religion. Matthew again and again points out places in the New Testament story that can be seen as fulfillments of the Old Testament. The Sermon on the Mount begins with the beatitudes, and we recall the earlier ten commandments, also delivered from a mountain. The division of Matthew into five sections, each beginning with a distinctive discourse of Jesus, suggests a new version of the Pentateuch, the first five books of the Bible.

But this attempt to relate Christianity to the old law had very practical value. There is evidence that the Christian freedom that Paul had defended was beginning to degenerate into lawlessness and complacency. Jewish persecution of the Christians had begun alongside the Roman, and everything pointed to the need to see the new covenant as a fulfillment of the old, to stress the new righteousness as not less but more demanding than the old. So in Matthew we can see the struggling church beginning to live its life of discipline and danger in a hostile world. To Mark's message of a new Gospel of salvation, Matthew adds the further emphases on the new law and the new community of believers.

Let us now turn to the contents of the two gospels. The events they describe are claimed by Christians to be not only human occurrences, but also, taken together, a single drama that is God's gift of salvation to man. But we dare not claim that they mean this to us until we have observed, as carefully as we can, what they meant to the participants and to the authors.

I. The Infancy Narrative in Matthew

Chapters 1-2

1. the genealogy of Jesus, 1:1-17 (compare Luke's version in 3:23-38)

Matthew's purpose here is clearly to establish the authentic messiahship of Jesus. He is descended from Abraham, who in faith originally responded to the call of God; and also from David, marking him as the fulfillment of the hope that the Messiah would spring from David's line. Yet see Matthew 22:41-46, where Jesus seems to reject a messiahship descended from David. Notice also the curious presence of women in Matthew's list: Ruth, a non-Jewess, and Rahab and Bathsheba, whose moral characters were not exactly of the best. Luke's list, often differing in detail, differs mainly in going back not merely to the start of Israel's history but to the very beginning of time itself, to Adam. Jesus, Luke seems to say, is not only the fulfillment of the messianic hope, he is part of God's plan from the beginning of creation. The problem of reconciling these genealogies has often exercised scholars: some say that Luke gives Mary's lineage, while Matthew gives Joseph's; some distinguish between Jesus' legal descent (Matthew) and his physical descent (Luke). But we should not linger too long over the task of reconciling the lists; the main function of both is to relate Jesus' appearance to the historic events of Old Testament history. It is difficult, furthermore, to see how a genealogy could have any meaning if the virgin birth tradition is accepted. Verse 16, which has many variant readings in the manuscripts, probably read like this in the original, before Matthew adapted it: "Jacob was the father of Joseph the husband of Mary; Joseph was the father of Jesus who is called Christ."

2. the birth, 1:18-25

"Betrothal" is not technically marriage, but it is very close to it in Jewish law, so Joseph is called "husband" in verse 19. According to law, Joseph could have taken the issue to the courts, but instead he decided to settle the matter privately by a divorce. The appearance of the angel changes his mind. Matthew here quotes the decisive passage in Isaiah 7:14 from the Greek translation of the Old Testament (the so-called Septuagint). The Greek word *parthenos* usually, but not always, means "virgin" in the Greek Old Testament; the Hebrew original, *almah* cannot mean "virgin," so we must conclude that Isaiah does not have a supernatural birth in mind. But Matthew here is interested in showing that Jesus is not only the Son of David, and thus the Messiah (through his legal descent from Joseph), but also the supernatural Son of God—not just from his baptism, as Mark 1:11 suggests, but from his birth. This is the reason the church used the Old Testament passage in this way. It should be noted that Luke and Matthew alone use the virgin birth to portray the divinity of Christ. Mark, John, and Paul, all equally concerned to call Jesus the Son of God, do not make use of this tradition. The evidence for it in Matthew and Luke is sufficient neither for its denial nor for its affirmation as an actual happening. Notice that verse 25 makes difficult the Roman idea of the perpetual virginity of Mary, and fits in with the mention of Jesus' brothers and sisters in Matthew 13:55-56 and the parallel in Mark 6:3.

3. the visit of the wise men, 2:1-12

Luke, like Matthew, mentions Jesus' birth in Bethlehem, but otherwise the two accounts differ somewhat. In Matthew, Jesus is apparently born in Joseph's house (verse 11); in Luke he is born in a stable. Here, we read nothing about the visit of the shepherds or about the census that brought Joseph and Mary from Nazareth to Bethlehem. Here, we read of the flight to Egypt; in Luke, the family returned to Nazareth (2:39).

This conflicting evidence has led some to question the historical basis of Jesus' birth in Bethlehem, and to point out that it would be natural for primitive Jewish Christians to use the enigmatic saying of Micah 5:2 as a prediction. Throughout his life, Jesus is always referred to as a Nazarene.

But the symbolism of the story stands, quite apart from the historical questions. The Magi were probably Babylonian astrologers, and the church has been right in reading this story as one concerning the relevance of Jesus to the Gentile world as well as to the Jewish world. Sometimes ancient records have been examined for a natural explanation of the moving star (in 7 B.C. there was a conjunction of Jupiter and Saturn, and in 12 B.C. a record of a comet), but it is not necessary to find this kind of evidence for the event. Matthew here is saying that all of nature is transformed by this unique birth. Later Christian thought found symbolic meanings in the three gifts: gold for Christ's royalty; incense for his priesthood; and myrrh for his burial; but here the gifts are simply appropriate to his status as the new king.

4. the conclusion of the story, 2:13-23

Egypt is close to Bethlehem, and there were many Jewish communities there. So there is nothing improbable about the journey here described. But the trip is probably suggested by Hosea 11:1, and further by the tendency in Matthew to see Jesus as a new Moses and lawgiver.

We need to be very careful in our observations of the way the New Testament writers see the story of Jesus in Old Testament patterns and terms. They may add details, but they are deeply convinced that what was going on in Jesus Christ was in fact a fulfillment of Old Testament hopes. Jesus, they are saying, comes into a world prepared by the Old Testament longings and hopes, and his story is the answer to those longings. However we may decide on the historical probability of particular details of the fulfillment of the Old Testament in the New, the fact of that fulfillment and the intimate relation of the Old and New Testaments cannot be surrendered.

In these stories, then, we see two motives at work. First, the desire to show that in the early life of the Messiah there are exact fulfillments of Old Testament predictions; second, the defense of the messiahship of Jesus against Jewish slanders that he was illegitimate and the son of an immoral woman. The miraculous birth seems designed to meet the second point; the birth at Bethlehem, the visit of the wise men, and the flight to Egypt, refer to the first.

II. The Infancy Narrative in Luke

Chapters 1-2

1. prologue, 1:1-4

Introductions like this one are very common in writings of this time, and this ought to be taken as introducing both this gospel and the book of the Acts. If Theophilus was a Gentile intellectual who had heard of Christianity, but who was not yet convinced, some of Luke's special emphases have a special relevance. The questions that such a man might ask are just the questions that concern Luke: Why did the Jews reject Jesus? If Judaism is discredited, why not Christianity as well?

2. the birth stories, 1:5—2:40, with a brief story about Jesus at the age of twelve, 2:41-52

If Theophilus was struggling between faith and doubt, the tension between faith and doubt in this section becomes especially interesting. Note the doubt of Zechariah in 1:18 and of Mary in 1:34. Already Luke creates an atmosphere of mystery: just who is this child?

a. the annunciation to Mary, 1:26-38

Notice that the miraculous character of the birth is directly stressed only in verse 34; apart from this the angel could be referring to a child born in the normal way. Belief in the miraculous conception (virgin birth as it is usually called) is derived from this story, and from Matthew 1:18-25 (see page 18). We have already noted the relevant factors in a decision on this matter. Luke clearly affirms it here, though he has not shaped all of his material consistently with that belief. (See Luke 2:48, and the genealogy which traces Jesus' lineage through Joseph.) It is important to point out that the belief was used in the early church as a way of affirming Jesus' full humanity; "born of a virgin" in the Apostles' Creed has the force of "really born of a woman," in opposition to heretics who denied that Jesus was truly human. The belief is defended on other theological grounds today: that it points to the fact that God's gift of himself to man is wholly grace, without human initiative. This of course is deeply true, whether one uses the story to emphasize it or not.

b. Mary visits Elizabeth, 1:39-56

Hearing of Elizabeth's similar good fortune, Mary journeys to visit her. In Luke 1:41-42, Elizabeth's unborn son is said to be aware of the reality of the unborn Messiah, and this awareness is transferred to Elizabeth herself. Mary's "Magnificat," beginning with verse 46, is a hymn, probably used in the early church, praising the mighty acts of God. It has been called the most revolutionary document in the world. It certainly must be cited to those who are sure that all religion is an opiate for the people.

c. the birth of John the Baptist, 1:57-80

Any birth, but especially the birth of a son, was an occasion for great rejoicing. The name is given, and Zechariah is released from his punishment (1:20). His song, known as the "Benedictus," is a hymn of praise to God for the birth of his son, the forerunner of the Messiah and the new age of forgiveness and peace. This hymn seems partly Luke's own composition, partly the reflection of many Old Testament passages.

d. Jesus' birth, 2:1-20

Matthew had assumed that Joseph and Mary had their regular residence in Bethlehem. Luke locates their home in Nazareth, but brings them to Bethlehem, a journey of eighty miles, for the census. The question, however, of the actual birthplace of Jesus is historically interesting, but has no religious significance.

Luke tries to date the event with precision. Caesar Augustus ruled from 27 B.C. to A.D. 14. We know that beginning in A.D. 20, censuses (for the purposes of levying taxes and registration for military service, in general; but the Jews were exempt from military service, and so we can assume that the former purpose alone applies here) were held every fourteen years until about A.D. 270. Therefore, if the fourteen-year cycle was in operation at this time, we can estimate the date of Jesus' birth to be about 8 B.C. There is one problem to this date; Quirinius did not become the actual governor of Syria until A.D. 6, but we do know that he held an official post in the area between 10 and 7 B.C., and so the date of 8 B.C. can perhaps stand.

"Betrothed" in Luke 2:5 may originally have read "wife," and have been later altered to fit in with 1:27. A manger is a place where animals feed, and it can mean either the barn itself or the actual feeding trough.

The narrative of the shepherds is full of interest. That sheep were grazing gives us the only clue we have for the actual season of the birth. In the third century, some parts of the church celebrated Christmas on January 6, but during the following century the date was settled on December 25, the traditional date of a pagan festival of rebirth. But sheep were kept in the field between the months of April and November, and apart from this we really have very little evidence on which to base an accurate dating. Shepherds were ordinarily outside the Jewish law, and considered quite an unrespectable class.

The heavenly hosts are the angels surrounding the throne of God. This entire section should indeed be treasured, but as the poetry, not the prose, of faith. If the birth was actually accompanied by such supernatural signs, it would be difficult to explain the later skepticism toward Jesus on the part of his family (see Mark 3:21, 31-32, and Luke 2:50).

e. circumcision and presentation in the temple, 2:21-40

Two separate Jewish rites are described, though not carefully distinguished: the circumcision of the infant and the purification of the mother. This whole passage stresses the intimate connection between Judaism and Christianity. "The consolation of Israel" in Luke 2:25 refers to fulfillment of the messianic hopes. Note the surprise of the parents at Simeon's prediction. This suggests that this material comes from a tradition that did not know either the virgin birth or the angel's announcement. Or, perhaps, the surprise may be that the Messiah is to save all people, Gentile and Jew.

f. Jesus at the age of twelve, 2:41-52

Luke's concern in this familiar story may be to stress Jesus' early interest in religious questions. But the real clue lies in verses 49-51, where a tension between his obedience to his (heavenly) Father and his parents is suggested. Jesus' response to his parents is not fully understood by them, but he obeys, and returns home. With this passage a basic tension in the entire gospel is set up: that between Sonship and suffering. Jesus here is both the son of his parents, and God's unique Son. Luke is more interested in this theological tension than in the details of the boyhood, and this is perhaps the reason that this is the only material we have on Jesus' youth.

III. The Ministry in Galilee According to Matthew and Luke

In this section we shall be dealing with some of the material in Matthew, Chapters 3 through 18; and in Luke, 3:1—9:50. This is parallel to the first nine chapters of Mark. By noting the biblical references following the paragraph titles, the reader will be able to distinguish between what Luke alone has, what Matthew alone has, what Luke and Matthew have in common, and what they take from Mark.

1. John the Baptist, Matthew 3:7-21 and Luke 3:7-20 (compare Mark 1:1-8)

a. his preaching of repentance, Matthew 3:7-10 and Luke 3:7-9

Mark merely refers to John's preaching of repentance, but Matthew and Luke give us an example of it. The message is prophetic, and John compares the hearers to snakes fleeing from a forest fire. There will be no privileged position for the Jews as children of Abraham, for God does not need them. The time of judgment and decision is now.

b. his messianic preaching, Matthew 3:11-12 and Luke 3:10-18

Matthew and Luke both have John point beyond himself to a greater one who will follow him, one who will baptize not with water but with the Spirit. In 3:10-14, Luke adds some of John's ethical teaching, but it seems perfunctory and not particularly demanding, especially when compared to Jesus' teaching on wealth and on love of enemies.

2. Jesus' baptism, Matthew 3:13-17 and Luke 3:21-22 (compare Mark 1:9-11)

Notice that while Mark clearly states that John baptized Jesus, Luke does not specifically say so, and Matthew feels some need (3:14-15) to explain why a sinless Christ should submit to a baptism requiring repentance. Three decisive points are made in the three images here: the heavens are opened; the Spirit descends, giving Jesus power to perform his work; and the voice of God speaks, defining Jesus as a unique Son of God.

3. Jesus' temptation, Matthew 4:1-11 and Luke 4:1-13 (compare Mark 1:12-13)

This is probably a description that Jesus gave to his disciples of his inner struggles about the meaning of his messiahship. Apart from the fact that the order of the second and third temptation differs in Matthew and Luke, their accounts are similar. No doubt about the messiahship is expressed, but only the temptation to have it take an easy and successful form: to become a mere provider of bread and physical need; to be a mere wonderworker and so to coerce people into belief; or to become a political messiah claiming sovereignty over the nations of the earth. We have already noted that as early as Luke 2:41-52 the tension between suffering and Sonship is present; here the problem is the acceptance of a messiahship without suffering. This struggle must be seen as a real one, and one that was costly and difficult to overcome. Matthew follows his temptation story with a brief description of Jesus' first teaching (4:17, compare Mark 1:15), having first pointed to Jesus' fulfillment of a saying from Isaiah 9:1-2. Luke simply indicates that Jesus returned from the wilderness and began to teach (4:14-15).

4. the rejection at Nazareth, Luke 4:16-30

Instead of including at this point a summary of Jesus' message, as Matthew did, Luke illustrates Jesus at work.

Synagogue worship included a regular reading from the law (which was required to be read through every three years) and reading and exposition of the prophets. Jesus is invited to read and expound from the prophets. "The acceptable year of the Lord" in the prophet's words referred to the future; Jesus here proclaims that this messianic age is now at hand, fulfilled in his own person. The popular response in Luke 4:20 begins with admiration, and ends in perplexity and hostility. Verses 23-27 are confusing, but apparently the Old Testament references are designed to meet the objection that Jesus should have performed his acts of healing in his own native village. Verse 30 implies a miraculous escape.

Many of the motifs of Luke's whole two-volume work are contained in this narrative: the Old Testament background of Jesus' message; thc Gospel preached to the poor; the arrival of the messianic age, the hostility of the Jews to his message, and their final rejection of him, climaxed by a miraculous act of deliverance.

5. the call of the disciples, Matthew 4:18-22 (compare Mark 1:16-20)

The theme of the Gospel is announced in Matthew 4:17, and to carry out its purpose, Jesus calls together a group. Note the startling immediacy of their response.

6. a group of healings, Luke 4:31-43 (compare Mark 1:21-38)

At this point Luke, though not Matthew, introduces a group of healing stories as a description of the power of the new Gospel that Jesus is proclaiming. The man in the synagogue (4:31-37) who has an unclean spirit seems to recognize Jesus as the Son of God.

Jesus heals Peter's mother-in-law (Luke 4:38-39), and later in the evening when the Sabbath was officially over and the Jews could approach Jesus without fear, he heals others (verses 40-41). The next morning he withdraws for prayer, as is his custom, but he is interrupted. There is a striking note of urgency and even impatience here, but there is the deeper hint that the work of preaching is more important than that of healing. Notice in verse 43 that Jesus declares himself to have been sent by God only for the purpose of preaching the Gospel of the kingdom.

7. the miraculous catch of fish, Luke 5:1-11

This is somewhat confusing, for we have a very similar story in John 21:4-14, which concerns the risen Christ and serves as a highly symbolic prediction of the ultimate success of the Christian mission. Here Luke sets aside any symbolic meaning, and uses the story as his version of the call of the disciples. It is hard to know if the story was originally a postresurrection one; here, in any case, it is the description of the response of Peter, James, and John, to Jesus' invitation.

8. the Sermon on the Mount, Matthew 5:1—7:29; and the Sermon on the Plain, Luke 6:20-49

Matthew and Luke have both collected a number of instances of Jesus' teaching, and placed them at this strategic point in their gospels. We need not suppose that this material was delivered at a single time or place. A word might be said about the kind of ethical teaching we have here. What is the relation of this teaching to the ordinary moral practices of society? Today people are always saying that their business practices, their foreign policies, their personal lives, are based on the Sermon on the Mount. Are we supposed to act in the ways indicated here? Are lawbreakers never to be punished, wars never to be fought, beggars to be given money indiscriminately? Jesus demands conduct without any thought of reciprocity; he demands perfection (Matthew 5:48). This demand is not based on what others might do, on practicability, or on consequences, but on what God has done and on what He is like. This body of teaching does not precisely answer the question: What am I to do in society? The question it answers is, What is God's absolute and radical will?

So even if this is impracticable in a law-court sense, it is binding. That is to say, nothing short of it is God's will. It is more like a compass than a map.

a. who is the citizen of the kingdom, and what is he like? (Matthew 5:1-16 and Luke, scattered)

1. the beatitudes (Matthew 5:3-12, Luke 6:20-23) and the woes (Luke 6:24-26)

In both Matthew and Luke, the teaching is addressed to the disciples. The beatitudes, and all the descriptions of the new man contained here, are meant to describe what God's will is for one who has chosen the kingdom of God, now breaking in upon men. We must read this today both as a judgment and a description of the Christian.

Luke has four beatitudes, Matthew nine; and Luke adds four woes, direct opposites of his blessings. Note that Luke refers to actual poverty and hunger, while Matthew has spiritualized the words. "Blessed" means "happy," or even, more exactly, "congratulations to the poor. . . ." It has been suggested that Matthew's list can be divided into three parts: Matthew 5:3-5 indicating three contrasts with the world's standards; verses 6-9 as positive traits of the Christian life; and verses 10-12 showing the world's inevitable reaction to this new quality introduced into it.

2. the relation of the disciple or the citizen of the kingdom to the world (Matthew 5:13-16, and Luke 14:34-35 and 11:33)

The disciple is not irrelevant to the world, he is like salt. This does not mean that he adds a little spice to the world, though there is nothing wrong with this idea in itself. In the ancient world salt was mainly a preservative, something to keep meat, for example, from spoiling. The disciple is the clue to the world, the supreme value the world possesses. Compare Matthew 5:14 with John 8:12—can both these be true?

Matthew 5:16 is sometimes, alas, used in Protestant churches as a prelude to the collection, but it contains the whole secret of Christian ethics. Your light must shine, of course; the Christian life is a visible one. But it must shine in a certain way, so that when men see your goodness they do not remark how good a person you are, but how great God is. And this is the problem: How do we do a good work so that *our* goodness is not noted by others, but only God's goodness? To call attention to our goodness is exactly what is forbidden here.

b. the new law and the old, Matthew 5:17-48

1. the key to this section, Matthew 5:17-20

Jesus is not destroying the Old Testament law as the contemporary scribes are interpreting it. He means to fulfill it, to fill it full of its true and absolute meaning, to show what it really involves. To illustrate, he takes six scribal interpretations of the Old Testament and interprets each in such a way as to show what it really means for the disciple, the citizen of the kingdom, the Christian.

2. on murder, Matthew 5:21-26 (compare Luke 12:57-59)

Jesus' meaning and method can be expressed in a paraphrase. "You have been hearing the scribes say that the Old Testament commandment against murder can be fulfilled if you avoid the act of violence that society calls murder. But I tell you that the inner disposition of the heart that leads to murder is really what is prohibited here: anger, irritation, the temptation to say to someone else, 'you fool.' Do not think that your conscience is clear if you have avoided murder. The inner meaning of this commandment is that all anger that elevates you and lowers another is forbidden by God." In other words, God regards anger against one's fellow man as serious an offense as man regards murder. Here the law in Jesus' hands is a surgical instrument, probing the human heart for any trace of egotism or pride.

3. on adultery, Matthew 5:27-30 (compare 18:8-9)

Jesus continues in effect: "The scribes tell you that the commandment against adultery is kept if you avoid the overt act of adultery. But I say that the inner lust of the heart after another is at the root of the adulterous act, and that this is forbidden by God." Adultery is a form of pride, and again this basic flaw is exposed here. This, someone has said, makes adulterers of us all. Jesus probes beneath the outer act to the inner meaning. "Don't commit adultery" means "Don't lust."

4. on divorce, Matthew 5:31-32

In the Old Testament it was possible for a man to put his wife away simply by writing out a document and giving it to her. Jesus says here that God's absolute will is that marriage should be indissoluble. It is probable that the phrase "except on the grounds of unchastity" is a later addition to soften Jesus' original words. See Mark 10:10-12, where Jesus' actual teaching on divorce is doubtless preserved. Compare with these also Matthew 19:9 and Luke 16:18.

5. on perjury, Matthew 5:33-37

This does not refer to profanity, but to lying under oath. The scribes have said that you must tell the truth when you are under oath. But oaths are required by law because society knows that all men are liars when their own interests are concerned. So, Jesus says, the scribal law is based on the assumption that all men are liars, and therefore it is not radical enough. Truth is demanded of the disciple whether he is under oath or not. He doesn't need special oaths to guarantee his word.

6. on retaliation, Matthew 5:38-42 (see Luke 6:29-30)

The scribes say that limited retaliation is possible. If you lose an eye in a fight, you may take one eye from the one who injured you. But Jesus says, do not resist evil at all. The old law says limited retaliation is permissible; Jesus says retaliation is itself evil. Perhaps something like this is behind the analysis. The old law of retaliation, called the *lex talionis,* was made to limit the taking of revenge: only one eye taken for one eye lost, one tooth for one tooth. This law is made to curb human sin, for it assumes that man will, if left alone, take greater vengeance than was taken on him. But since retaliation has to be curbed by the law, it is proved to be evil. Therefore the true spirit of the law is: don't retaliate, don't be vindictive.

An interesting question to raise is this: Does this analysis apply only to a man-to-man relation? What happens when more than two are involved? If someone hits you, do you lead him to a friend of yours so that he can hit him as well? Does the introduction of a third party alter the character of the law? Is pacifism a necessary consequence of this?

7. on love of enemies (Matthew 5:43-48; see Luke 6:27-36)

The scribes were teaching that a sort of fence can be put around the word "neighbor" in such a way that those outside the fence could be called enemies. Those inside are to be loved, those outside hated, or at best, ignored. But this, Jesus says, is not the meaning of the word neighbor. Your neighbor is anyone who has a claim on you; he is everyone, and there are no enemies for the disciple (except, perhaps, in the unimportant sense of those who are hostile to you—but even this is no excuse for the disciple to refuse to serve them, for who needs love more than the loveless and hostile?).

Matthew 5:45 and Luke 6:35 state the ground for Christian love with unmistakable clarity. Note that it does not say that we should love our enemies because it is the best policy and because the power of our love might win them to our position. Nor does it say that every man has an inherent value, however deeply concealed, which our love might fan into flame. Jesus does not allow our love to depend on perceived value in the neighbor. It may be there, it may not. We are to love because we are sons of God, and he loves his children universally, regardless of their human merits or traits. The shape and direction of our love is to be that of God's love for us.

The reader may want to follow up this point. Turn first to another important definition of the neighbor in the familiar parable of the Good Samaritan in Luke 10:29-37; (see page 53). Note also the key passages in the New Testament that define the quality of God's love; if our love for one another depends on his love for us, we must get very clear the nature of that love. Romans 5:8, I Corinthians 13, Ephesians 5:1-2, and I John 4:7-12, all bear special relevance to Jesus' teaching on love here.

c. spiritual discipline in the kingdom, Matthew 6:1-18

In the previous section Jesus has analyzed six scribal interpretations of the law. Here he takes three typical virtues of the Pharisees: almsgiving, prayer, and fasting, and shows how easy it is to do good for the wrong reasons.

1. almsgiving, Matthew 6:1-4

Apparently the Pharisees assumed that it was possible to gain favor in the sight of God by giving money to the poor. Jesus takes the idea of almsgiving, with all its dangers of self-display, and removes all merit from it. If you do this, he says, to gain a reward, you will get one—the praise of men, and that is all. Do good of course, but say nothing about it. It is possible, and fatally easy, to do good acts sinfully. Compare Luke 11:37-53, which is also a controversy with the Pharisees based on the question of alms.

2. prayer, Matthew 6:5-15 (see Luke 11:2-4 for another version of the Lord's Prayer, given in a different context. See page 54)

Here Jesus again points to the self-display of the Pharisees who liked to be seen praying in public. Their piety shall be seen by men, and that is all the reward they receive. He asks his disciples to retire into the pantry (that is really the word in Matthew 6:6) and to pray quietly there.

A few questions can be raised about the content of the Lord's Prayer. "Our Father" is one of the very rare instances in the New Testament where Jesus invited all men to consider God as their Father. For the most part, Jesus is *the* Son, and God is *his* Father. Perhaps we cannot really know that God is Father until we come to him through the Son.

"Hallowed be thy name": God's name is his very nature, and that nature is holy and majestic, beyond men. Let thy kingdom now come, Jesus prays, and adds to explain the meaning, let thy will be done here and now on earth. The kingdom's present reality is as fully stressed here as is its future completion. Notice the frank concern for the physical needs of men. Give us enough food for the day; the necessities of life are as "religious" as the more exalted spiritual gifts.

Note the close relationship between human and divine forgiveness here. Can man be forgiven by God if he is himself unforgiving? But can man ever make himself forgiving enough to deserve God's forgiveness? "Temptation" means a situation in which a Christian is tempted to recant or minimize his faith. If it be thy will, Jesus asks, do not lead us into the dangers and crises of life; but when they come, he goes on, keep us from succumbing to evil.

The conclusion to the prayer, "for thine is the kingdom . . ." is not found in the best manuscripts of Matthew and Luke, and is either an independent later piece of oral tradition, or a liturgical conclusion which the church added when the prayer came to be used in worship.

3. fasting, Matthew 6:16-18

The ostentatious fasting of the Pharisees is now under scrutiny.

When you undergo any form of self-discipline, Jesus says, do it gladly and keep it to yourself.

d. simplicity and carefreeness in the kingdom, Matthew 6:19-34

Jesus here turns to the external things that God gives to man for his enjoyment: food, drink, clothes, property. The best word to sum up the Christian attitude to these things is *detachment*. Unlike some religions, Christianity does not condemn these things, but points out that they can readily be misused. To put God and his kingdom first (Matthew 6:33, Luke 12:31) is to be ready to forego, at any time, any of these lesser goods. We must not be anxious about them, for to trust in them too absolutely is to betray our trust in God. These lesser goods can easily become substitute gods for us if concern for them controls the whole of our lives. (It might be noted, however, that there is a vast moral difference between the secure man's overconcern with his possessions and the unemployed man's anxiety about his lack of these goods. The wealthy man preaching the virtues of poverty to the poor, on the grounds that God will provide, represents a special kind of immorality.)

1. God and mammon, Matthew 6:19-24

Often, Jesus suggests, we accumulate possessions because of our fear of the future. But these things fall apart, they can be stolen, and many new toys soon bore us. Instead of being a form of security, they can become an added worry. Matthew 6:21 suggests the interesting idea that we can be known, and can know ourselves, by observing what we would least rather do without, what we would give the most to get. "Mammon" means possessions of any kind; owning them is not opposed here, but serving them is. Often things we think we control end up by controlling us. Verse 24 means that it is impossible to give absolute loyalty to two principles, just as it is impossible for a man to be in love with two women at the same time, if love has any real meaning at all.

2. freedom from fear, Matthew 6:25-34 (Luke 12:22-31)

Anxiety has sometimes been called the root of all sin. If we are anxious about our self-esteem, we shall often assert ourselves in a proud way over others. Here Jesus probes to the heart of this problem. He says: Do not be anxious at all. The reason is not that it is psychologically harmful or that there are not good reasons for it (there is always reason for it, and there is probably always room for the right kind of anxiety or concern about ourselves and the world). We are not to be fundamentally anxious before God because he is to be trusted, and will care for his people. Verse 34 reminds us that the worries of tomorrow won't be the ones we expected anyway. So let us face just the present day with trust in God.

e. judging and asking in the kingdom, Matthew 7:1-12

1. on judging, Matthew 7:1-5 (Luke 6:37-42)

In this chapter, we return to a note that we have already seen in Chapter 6: opposition to hypocrisy, perhaps the most important single element in Jesus' ethical teaching. The argument in Matthew 7:1-2 is highly compressed. Don't judge, in order that you won't be judged (by God). Why shouldn't we want to be judged? Because we shall be judged by the same standards that we use to judge others. And we could not survive that ordeal and be vindicated, for we have no merits of our own with which we could meet God's judgment. And so we are not to judge, because we could never hope to survive the judgment of God. Man's natural inclination is to judge himself very leniently, and others very harshly. The disciple is one who reverses this order. For an interesting application of this, see John 7:53—8:11 (printed as a footnote in the RSV).

Matthew 7:6 is an apparently irrelevant interlude. This may be an indication of Matthew's anti-Gentile bias, and "dogs" may refer to the non-Jew.

2. on asking, Matthew 7:7-12 (see Luke 11:9-13)

These familiar words contain a revolutionary idea: that "everyone" who asks will receive. This runs quite counter to the prevailing Old Testament view that God listened only to the righteous (see Psalm 34:15 ff.) Here Jesus notes that God listens even to the undeserving, and gives to all who ask, not perhaps what they will, but in accordance with his will. Is there such a thing as unanswered prayer? Notice also the interesting analogy in Matthew 7:11. Man, who is evil, can perform occasional acts of kindness; how much more can God who is good give to those who ask.

Matthew 7:12 (and Luke 6:31), often called the Golden Rule, is based on the previous verse which stressed what God does even for the undeserving. Since God acts in this way to us, there is only one basis for our actions toward others: putting ourselves in the other's place. Here is a rule of thumb for the disciple in any action: reverse the roles of self and other; you will discover by this that he too is a man in need. Then base your action on the insight gained from this identification. This is not so much a principle or an ideal to be applied (perhaps we talk too much about applying Christian ideals) but an invitation to identify yourself with the concrete concerns of another.

f. the kingdom and the two ways, Matthew 7:13-23

1. the narrow gate, Matthew 7:13-14 (Luke 13:23-24)

It is difficult to be sure just what "destruction" means here. Is this eternal judgment in hell, or merely the spiritual destruction of being without God? The disciple, in any case, will always be a minority. This passage has always been a barrier to ideas of universal salvation.

2. the danger of false prophets, Matthew 7:15-23 (see Luke 6:43-46, 13:26-27)

Do not be beguiled by a teacher's external appearance, Jesus says, or even by his words. Look at the effects of his words in his life: this is the real means of judging. In Matthew 7:21 we see again a favorite idea of Jesus: people who mouth the conventional words are not necessarily true disciples. A man must go beyond intentions and words to acts, to the demanding discipline of doing the will of God.

g. conclusion, Matthew 7:24-29 (see Luke 6:47-49)

1. how to respond to the "sermon," Matthew 7:24-27

Here again the perils of a merely verbal religion are stressed. Hearing must be followed by doing and obedience.

2. Matthew's editorial conclusion, Matthew 7:28-29

The crowds were astonished, yet in 5:1-2 it seemed as if only the disciples were being addressed. In point of fact, Matthew intends this sermon as instruction for all Christians, though in Jesus' own time only the disciples had committed their lives to him in such a way that the teaching could be relevant to them. They were astonished, for he spoke with power and authority.

For the Christian, this is the Son of God who has spoken, and his teachings here are an act of radical judgment on the world. No wonder the hearers were astonished and upset.

9. the healing of a leper, Matthew 8:1-4 and Luke 5:12-16 (compare Mark 1:40-45)

When Mark writes up this incident he mentions Jesus' pity for the man. For some reason, Matthew and Luke both omit this human touch.

A word might be said here about these healing stories; this is the first one in a series, and we shall come up against many similar stories in the two gospels we are studying. Demon-possession is the way biblical man explained what we would call physical and mental illness. Sometimes the healings are to be seen as signs of the coming kingdom of heaven (see Matthew 12:28); sometimes they are marks of Jesus' very human concern for the physical as well as the spiritual part of man. But a modern reader will want to ask, "Did they happen?" as well as "What do they mean?" However devout we may feel ourselves to be, it is not easy to accept such things. Some try to explain the healings by Jesus' power of suggestion, believing that the diseases were what we would call psychosomatic. And some of the stories may yield to this approach. Some, like the story of the Gadarene demoniac (Matthew 8:28-34), may well have a good deal of legendary material attached to them. And readers will doubtless want to raise the whole question of spiritual healing in this connection. But, remember, the main clue to our interpretation of these difficult pieces of material is this: what and who do we believe Jesus Christ to be? If he was in fact what the Christian tradition has tried to claim, then we cannot be certain that such things cannot happen.

10. the centurion's servant, Matthew 8:5-13 and Luke 7:1-10

Fearing that Jesus would not wish to enter a Gentile house, the centurion in Matthew's narrative says that since he is a soldier and knows the meaning of authority, Jesus can merely speak a word of power, and the healing will be accomplished. This confidence elicits

Jesus' praise, and the servant is healed. In verses 11-12, Matthew has drawn out the missionary implications of the Gentile's faith by means of a figure taken from the idea of the messianic banquet in heaven. Luke uses this material, but in another context (13:28-30).

11. the widow's son, Luke 7:11-17

In his reply to John the Baptist, in Luke 7:22, Jesus declares that in his ministry the dead have been raised. This story, which Luke alone has, seems to be included to support that description. Stories of Jesus raising someone from the dead are fairly rare in the New Testament: the raising of Jairus' daughter may be such a story, but it is not entirely clear (see page 41); John 11:1-44 is another. These cannot but be stumbling blocks for us today, and perhaps they should be set aside until we deal with the chief stumbling block, the resurrection of Jesus himself. The symbolic meaning of the story is important to Luke: Jesus is both the bearer and the giver of new life.

12. on discipleship, Matthew 8:18-22 and Luke 9:57-62

Here are some descriptions of the nature of true discipleship. To the first inquirer (called a scribe by Matthew), Jesus points out the risks and insecurities of the disciple's lot. To the second, Jesus says that even the sacred duties of the law must be abandoned: those who allow their legal duties to stand in the way of full obedience are the truly dead ones, the spiritually dead. Luke adds a third point in 9:61-62: discipleship requires the same attention and care as does the plowing of a straight furrow.

13. the Gadarene madman, Matthew 8:28-34 and Luke 8:26-39 (compare Mark 5:1-20)

Matthew and Luke make their own use of this story from Mark.

Matthew radically shortens it, and cuts much of the detail that Luke includes. In Luke the madman greets Jesus, and begs him to leave him alone. He wryly tells Jesus that his name is Legion, a reference to the multitude of demons possessing him. Jesus calms the man, and news of the cure is spread about; the people from the countryside fear Jesus, perhaps because of the destruction of the swine, and beg him to leave. The man himself begs to go with Jesus, but Jesus refuses and sends him back to his village to announce to all what God has done.

14. healing the paralytic, Matthew 9:1-8 and Luke 5:17-26 (compare Mark 2:1-12)

This is another story taken over from Mark. Again Matthew shortens and simplifies. Luke has the man brought to Jesus by being lowered through the roof of a house where Jesus was teaching, surrounded by a crowd. The faith of those who bring the man is commended; Jesus forgives the paralytic's sins. This offends the scribes (and the Pharisees, Luke adds), for only God can forgive. Jesus affirms his status as the divine Son of man, authorized to bear the divine forgiveness, and bids the man to rise from his bed and walk. Two real miracles take place here; a man receives the divine forgiveness, and he is healed. Spiritual and physical needs are all of a piece, and both can be met by Jesus' word of healing.

15. the woman with a hemorrhage and Jairus' daughter, Matthew 9:18-26 and Luke 8:40-56 (compare Mark 5:21-43)

A ruler, in Matthew—a Jewish leader, in Luke—comes to Jesus and bids him come to his daughter. Matthew says she has died; Luke, that she is dying. Jesus follows the man, and on the way a woman with a chronic hemorrhage pushes through the crowd to touch Jesus. Luke says that Jesus felt a power go forth from him when she touched him. Matthew merely says that Jesus sees her, and declares that her faith has made her well. The party then arrives at Jairus' house. Matthew seems to play down the miracle; Jesus merely says that the girl is not dead but sleeping; he goes in, and the girl rises from her bed. In Luke, when they arrive at the house, the report comes that the girl has died, and they conclude that Jesus should therefore not be bothered. This suggests that Jesus was not expected to be able to raise the dead. Jesus takes Peter, James, John, and the girl's parents with him into the house. He calls the child, and she arises.

It is hard to know what is meant here by the saying of Jesus in both accounts that "she is not dead but sleeping." Does this mean that Jesus knew she was not truly dead? Or that death is not the true end of man? Was he making a diagnosis? Is this intended to be a raising from the dead? This is used, both by Luke and Matthew, as a sort of climax to a series of miracle stories, and it seems as if they treat it as a miracle of resurrection. But the details of the story are not entirely clear, and this perhaps is a place where some may wish to reserve judgment or even to doubt the event as it stands. In any case, beyond these details stands the deeper and more important truth about Jesus, that through him is new life, both now and in the world to come.

16. the sending of the disciples, Matthew 9:35—11:1 (compare Luke 9:1-6 and 10:1-12)

This might be called the second main discourse of Jesus to his disciples in Matthew, the first being the Sermon on the Mount. Between the two discourses, Matthew has placed some of the healing stories of Jesus to serve as a pattern for the Christian minister. Now the disciples are commissioned to leave their teacher and to go out into the world.

a. introduction, 9:35-38

Jesus' work of teaching (Matthew 5, 6, 7) and healing (8—9:34) is summarized, and the need for special apostles or representatives is described. Their work is compared to that of a shepherd gathering sheep or a harvester bringing in the grain.

b. the twelve, Matthew 10:1-4

The list of names is the same as that found in Mark.

c. the discourse of Jesus to the disciples, 10:5—11:1

In Matthew 10:5-15 Jesus describes the aim and manner of evangelism. The disciples are to go to Jews alone, and their words and work are to be the same as Jesus'. The paggage 10:16-39 is a collection of sayings, all centering around the idea of opposition and persecution. In Luke 10:17 we read that this original mission of the disciples was successful, and so here Matthew must be referring not to the fate of the disciples but to the fate of the church at the time of the writing of his gospel. The councils are the local Jewish bodies, and apparently punishment was often administered in the synagogue itself. Christians are advised to trust in God and not to prepare elaborate defenses. The details of verses 21-22 suggest an actual persecution, perhaps that of Nero around A.D. 65. This saying is formulated by Christians who believed both that Jesus was the supernatural Son of man, and that he would shortly return.

In Matthew 10:26-33 the church is exhorted to fearlessness in the face of danger and to trust in God, who cares for even the smallest things of earth. Verses 34-39 recognize that the claims of the Gospel may clash with other loyalties. Perhaps such divisions of families were actually taking place in the time of persecution.

The basic paradox and secret of the Christian life in verse 39 is given special power in this setting of actual persecution.

In Matthew 10:40—11:1, we move from the setting of the persecution of Christians back to the original context of Jesus' mission charge to the disciples. After some words on how to receive the disciples on their mission, and a commendation of simple acts of helpfulness, the discourse comes to a close.

17. the rejection of Jesus by the Jewish leaders, Matthew 11:2—12:50

After his presentation of the missionary function of the church, Matthew here describes the dramatic story of Jesus' rejection. There are three different sets of controversy here (11:2-19, 12:1-14, 12:22-37), with intervals of serenity intervening (11:25-30, 12:15-21 and 12:46-50).

a. Jesus and the question from John the Baptist, Matthew 11:2-19 and Luke 7:18-35

The first challenge to Jesus comes from John the Baptist. Is there a note of disappointment in his reported question? Had he expected more of the Messiah? He seems to wonder if Jesus is in fact the Messiah, for that is what "he who is to come" means. Jesus, in reply, points to what has been done, and Chapters 8 and 9 in Matthew have recorded these signs.

Jesus goes on (Matthew 11:7-19) to describe, to praise, and to identify John as the forerunner of the Messiah. Matthew 11:12-14 is difficult, for it is not clear if the interval between John and Jesus' teaching or between John and the early church is meant. In the first case, the violence would be that of the Jewish revolutionaries who tried to bring the kingdom to pass by force. In the second sense, the men of violence would be the earthly rulers who tried to prevent it. The little picture of verses 16-17 portrays two groups of children, one inviting the other to play—first, a dancing game, second, a weeping game. Both offers were rejected. Are John and Jesus those who offer and the rest of the people those who reject? Verses 18-19 suggest that the ascetic John may be compared to the children's offer of a weeping game, and that the non-ascetic Jesus, eating and drinking, may be compared to the dancing game. Jesus is identifying himself with John (both are being rejected) more than distinguishing himself. It is interesting that this section begins with John wondering whether Jesus should be rejected, and ends with Jesus portraying the world's rejection of both of them.

b. Jesus as revelation of God, Matthew 11:25-30 (Luke 10:21-22)

In verses 20-24, we have an instance of Jesus' rejection of those who are rejecting him, but with verse 25 we turn to quite a different mood. The section can be divided into three parts: verses 25-26, Jesus' thanksgiving to God; verse 27, Jesus declares himself to be the unique Son of God; (these three verses find an exact parallel in Luke 10:21-22); and verses 28-30, an appeal to follow, found only here in Matthew. Because verses 25-27 sound so much like the fourth gospel, considerable critical effort has been spent on a study of them. Some scholars can find no reason for questioning their authenticity as coming from Jesus; some describe them as an early inspired interpretation of Jesus, ascribed to him as defining his true meaning. Some effort must always be made to distinguish between sayings of Jesus before his death and "sayings" of the risen Lord to the church, though we should never be very certain of any distinction. If we believe that this saying is a true one about Jesus, then there is little to keep us from affirming that he could have easily said it of himself, even though this kind of self-description is rare in the synoptic gospels. To say that the Son alone "knows" the Father is not to say that we are all forced to be agnostics. But it does suggest that we do not know God fully, directly, or adequately. Our "knowing" is by faith, not by vision or touch or sight. And we know even the little that we do because of Jesus Christ, because he does "know" fully.

11:28 refers to those who labor and are heavy laden by the burden of the law which the scribes put upon men. Jesus' own interpretation of the law (Matthew 5—7) and of himself (verses 25-27 above) involves a new yoke but an easy one, in the wearing of which rest and peace are substituted for anxiety and fear. That this great passage should come in the midst of a context of Jesus' rejection by men reminds us how closely his rejection and death are tied to his gift of rest and peace.

c. further examples of the rising opposition to Jesus, Matthew 12:1-50

1. picking grain and healing on the Sabbath, Matthew 12:1-14

These stories may be read as examples of the new and lighter "yoke" described in verse 29 above. The first is from Mark 2:23-28, and is also used by Luke 6:1-5. The second is from Mark 3:1-6 (though you will note that Matthew has removed the reference to Jesus' anger), and Luke's version in 6:6-11 is very close to Matthew. Refer also to Luke 13:10-17 for further material on Jesus and the Sabbath. The issue in all these Sabbath controversies is that of the relation of human need to the law. When the law interferes with human well-being, it is to be broken, and Jesus' uncompromising position prompts the Pharisees to make plans to put him out of the way (Matthew 12:14 and Luke 6:11).

2. Jesus' withdrawal, Matthew 12:15-21

In spite of the growing hostility, Jesus continues his acts of healing. Matthew briefly summarizes Mark 3:7-12 and adds the interpretative quotation from one of the great servant songs (Isaiah 42:1-4) suggesting both that Jesus' greatness is his humiliation, and the fact that even though rejected by the Pharisees he would be known as the justice and the hope of the Gentiles.

3. *another healing and another controversy, Matthew 12:22-37 (compare Mark 3:19-30)*

Luke's version of this can be found in 11:14-23, 12:10, and 6:43-45. Notice that Matthew and Luke both omit the accusation by Jesus' family and friends that he is mad (Mark 3:21). The inclusion of Jesus' discourse in 12:33-37 is intended by Matthew as a bitter criticism of the Pharisees, who in condemning Jesus have really condemned themselves.

4. *the demand for a sign, Matthew 12:38-42 (Luke 11:29-32)*

Since Jesus has claimed to be inspired by the Spirit, some of the Jews ask for a decisive proof of his claim, perhaps a nice unambiguous miracle. But Jesus had already rejected that way in the temptation, so he refuses, saying that the only sign they will have is the sign of Jonah—the preaching of repentance. This is clearly the meaning of the sign of Jonah in Jesus' mind, but Matthew, like many other Christians since, can think only of the "whale" when he thinks of Jonah, and so he adds his own interpretation of the sign of Jonah, using the prophet's sojourn in the belly of the great fish as a symbol of the death and resurrection. Luke, note, does not add this flourish. Of course the true sign that is given all Christians *is* Christ's death and resurrection, and so we must say that Matthew has in a sense rightly interpreted the full meaning of Jesus' words, but in such a way as to make it harder to get at the original sense of the passage.

The citizens of Nineveh, who responded to Jonah's message, and the Queen of Sheba (who sought out Solomon, I Kings 10:1-

13) are wiser than the Pharisees, and will be present at the last judgment to condemn them for asking for more evidence than they need.

5. on exorcism, Matthew 12:43-45 (Luke 11:24-26)

These general remarks on exorcism are located here because the controversy originally began with an act of healing. Some traditional beliefs about demons are included, such as the fact that they do not like water. The Jewish nation is compared to the healed man who is in danger of sliding back into something worse than his original state.

6. Jesus' true family, Matthew 12:46-50 (Mark 3:13-15, Luke 8:19-21)

The point is seen in Matthew 12:50: Jesus' true family is not necessarily those who are in blood relationship to him (that is, the Jews), but those who obey him. Here in Matthew, it is the disciples who are the true family; in Mark, it is the whole crowd who was listening to him.

* * * * *

The two concluding sections (IV and V) in this guide deal first with some of Luke's characteristic material and, finally, with the close of the ministry as interpreted by both Matthew and Luke. But before we turn to these sections, some very brief notes on the intervening material follow.

1. Matthew 13:1-52 is a long collection of parables, including the parable of the sower (verses 1-9; see Luke 8:4-8) and an interpretation of it (Matthew 13:18-23 and Luke 8:11-15). Between the parable and its interpretation, Jesus tells his disciples why he uses the form of the parable for his teaching (Matthew 13:10-15 and Luke 8:9-10). Is Jesus saying that the

purpose of the parables is to confuse and to withhold the truth from the outsider? It may be that the outsiders do not in fact comprehend his message, but are the parables designed to obscure it? The verses from Isaiah 6:9-10 are a key here, and the reader may wish to turn to them in the context of the prophet's message. Luke 8:16-18 seems to suggest quite a different interpretation of the parables, from verses 9-10 just before. Mark 4:1-25 is the basis of this section. Matthew 13:24-30, 36-43 contains another parable and interpretation, that of the weeds and the wheat. Note the realistic conception of judgment and evil here and how 13:39-40 suggests that good and evil will grow together in history until the end of time. No inevitable historical progress in Jesus' teaching!

2. Matthew 14:1-12 (and more briefly Luke 9:7-9) records the death of John the Baptist and the return of the disciples from their mission. Matthew and Luke both include the feeding of the 5,000 (14:13-21 and 9:10-17; compare Mark 6:30-44), but Matthew alone follows Mark in including the second feeding of the 4,000 (15:32-39; compare Mark 8:1-10). The second story is sometimes referred to as a "doublet"; not a second incident, but a variant account of the earlier feeding. Matthew may have discerned a symbolic meaning to the two events: the first is on Jewish soil, and twelve baskets of food are left over (symbolic number?). The second is on Gentile soil, and the adequacy of Jesus' message to both Jew and Gentile may be the point here. It is hard to see why the disciples would have asked the question in Matthew 15:33 if a similar miracle had taken place shortly before. Matthew and Luke treat these stories as miracles, to be sure; but there is a meaning in them beyond their form. Notice Matthew 14:19, Luke 9:16, and Matthew 15:36. The action of blessing, breaking, and giving thanks reminds us of the last supper, and Matthew and Luke clearly invite us to look beyond the miracle to its meaning; that Jesus

Christ is fully adequate to all human need. Not even the disciples fully grasp this meaning in Matthew 16:5-12.

Matthew inserts an important bloc of material on defilement between the two feeding stories, 15:1-20, 15:11 is the key to the passage, and it is both a decisive blow against the external legalism of the Pharisees and an important passage for the field of Christian personal ethics.

3. Peter's confession of Jesus as the Messiah is a moment of decisive importance (Matthew 16:13-23 and Luke 9:18-22; compare Mark 8:27-33). Peter blurts out what many of the disciples must have been thinking, but what had not been openly stated. In Matthew, Jesus reminds Peter that his insight is not a human achievement, but a gift of God. Matthew 16:18-19 has been the source of much controversy, of course, for it is one of the bases of the claim of the Roman Catholic tradition that their ministry goes directly back to Peter. At times, some Protestant critics have denied that these are actual words of Jesus, though the tendency today is to see them as genuine. But what is the "rock" on which Jesus will build? Is it Peter himself, or is it Peter's confession that Jesus is the Messiah? There is no reason why Protestants should not say that Peter himself is the "rock." The church is in existence whenever sinful men declare Jesus' true meaning. The keys are apparently the power of forgiveness, and surely forgiveness is one of the chief functions of the Christian church as a whole, Protestant or Roman Catholic. But Jesus goes on to describe his coming suffering, and in Matthew (though not in Luke) Peter refuses to believe that the Messiah must suffer, and he is crushingly rebuked as a "Satan" by Jesus. And so, in one way, Peter hasn't really seen Jesus' meaning at all. The real center of this passage is perhaps not so much Peter, but the new and as yet misunderstood truth that the Messiah must suffer and die. The disciples will not really see this until after the resurrection.

4. Like the Messiah, the disciples too must expect suffering. Three

conditions for discipleship are set forth (Matthew 16:24-28 and Luke 9:23-27; compare Mark 8:34—9:1). The first is self-denial, the second is taking up the cross, and the third is following Jesus. These three conditions are really one, and together they mean radical obedience to Jesus Christ, the Messiah who is about to suffer and die.

Notice Matthew 16:28 and Luke 9:27 (compare Mark 9:1). What event is being referred to? The resurrection of Christ; Pentecost; or perhaps, in Matthew, some kind of "coming" of the Son of man that Jesus expected but that did not occur? Does Jesus refer to himself or to another in Matthew 16:28? See page 57 for Luke's treatment of the Son of man.

5. The transfiguration will repay careful study, and again we must carefully distinguish two questions: What actually happened? What is the meaning? (Matthew 17:1-8 and Luke 9:28-36; compare Mark 9:2-8). Some have called this an historical event in which the true glory of Christ is revealed to the disciples. Some have called it a subjective vision, some a mere legend, some a resurrection-appearance, here out of place. We cannot escape the kind of question that we as modern men and women put to material like this; and "did it happen?" is an appropriate thing to ask, even if this question would not have been wholly intelligible to Matthew or Luke. But beyond this, what event is being portrayed in the experience of the disciples? There are some touches that remind us of the baptism of Jesus, the voice from heaven for example; and it may be that this event is designed as a counterpart to the baptism in the minds of the disciples. Jesus knew who he was at baptism; his meaning was briefly glimpsed when Peter made his confession; now, the meaning is even more openly declared. As with Peter's confession, there is an emphasis on Peter's misunderstanding. He wants Moses (the law), Elijah (the prophets), and Jesus on the same level; Luke apologizes for Peter's foolishness (verse 33), and the voice from heaven corrects Peter's implied view

of the relation of Christ to the Old Testament. Here, as at the baptism, and at Peter's confession, something is seen, and something is withheld, about the meaning of Christ. It is by no means clear that the disciples discerned the meaning of this event.

Following this in Matthew and Luke is the healing of the epileptic boy (Matthew 17:14-21 and Luke 9:37-43); and a second prediction of his death by Jesus (17:22-23 and 9:43-45). There follows a strange saying about the temple tax in Matthew (17:24-27); an argument about true greatness (Matthew 18:1-5 and Luke 9:46-48); and some teaching material in Matthew, 18:6-35, concluding, in verses 23-35, with the superb parable of the unforgiving servant, a vivid and impressive study of the relation of human and divine forgiveness.

This brings us to the place in Luke where he introduces his special selection of material, and to this we now turn. Immediately after the incidents above, Matthew turns to the Passion narrative of Jesus' final days, and this we shall pick up in our final section V.

IV. Some Characteristic Material from Luke

Luke's special source contains some of the most beautiful and familiar material in the New Testament. His personal interests shine through, his parables are skillfully and forcefully told, and his trustworthiness as an historian is in evidence.

1. the woman with the ointment, Luke 7:36-50

Luke uses this story to elaborate the saying in 7:34 that Jesus is a glutton, and consorts with sinners. Jesus is invited to supper by a

Pharisee. A woman, probably a prostitute, breaks in and, weeping over him in remorse, bathes his feet with ointment. Simon had apparently first assumed that Jesus was a prophet with special powers of insight, and then concludes that he could not be so, since he did not discern the true character of the woman. Luke apparently suggests, however, that Jesus read Simon's thoughts (verse 40).

The little parable in Luke 7:41-42 does not really make the same point as the story makes. The story says that the woman, who loves much (her act of anointing is an act of love) is therefore forgiven, but that Simon is loveless and correct and therefore is not forgiven because he does not think he needs to be. But the parable says that one who is forgiven much, loves much. The first part of verse 47 summarizes the story; the second part summarizes the point of the parable. This story may be Luke's reworking of the anointing at Bethany in Mark 14:3-9. The main point of the story is, in spite of the parable, still clear. Jesus contrasts the ecstatic and spontaneous act of love of the broken woman with the formal and loveless correctness of the Pharisee; she will be forgiven, he will not.

2. the Good Samaritan, Luke 10:29-37

This is a special kind of parable, found only in Luke, in which we are given an example to imitate. Unlike Mark, where the parables mainly pointed to the meaning of the kingdom of God, here the story is told in answer to the question: "Who is the neighbor that I am supposed to love?" Notice how neatly Jesus turns the question around. The neighbor is not someone "out there," "anyone in need," as we might say. You are the neighbor, and to act as a neighbor is to act as the Samaritan did. The Samaritan was a layman, of mixed racial origin, outside the Jewish law, and hated and suspected by the pious Jew.

3. Mary and Martha, Luke 10:38-42

Martha complains that Mary neglects the duties of a hostess. Jesus defends Mary, setting her response before the merely technical and formal busyness of Martha. The true hostess of the Lord, we might say, is to attend carefully to his words. This need not be pressed to mean that going to church is more important than housework. The real contrast is between formal, proper (and in this case slightly petulant) correctness and reverent attention to the meaning of Jesus.

4. teaching on prayer, Luke 11:1-13

As we have already seen, Matthew (6:9-13) puts the Lord's Prayer in the Sermon on the Mount, as a contrast to the Pharisees' ostentatious praying. Here it is a response to a request for instruction. Luke's version of the text is shorter, and probably the original one. Matthew writes "as we also have forgiven our debtors"; Luke makes this more clear by "for we ourselves forgive everyone who is indebted to us."

The little parable in verses 5-8 is found only in Luke. Compare Luke 18:1-8. Only one point is intended in both parables; God is not to be compared to the lazy friend or the unjust judge. The lesson is this: if persistence works on the human level, how much more will it work in your prayer.

5. the parable of the rich fool, Luke 12:13-21

Rabbis often heard legal disputes, and the brother bringing the case to Jesus expected a favorable decision. But Jesus refuses to take the burden of decision from the men, and tells them in effect to make their own decision, avoiding covetousness. The parable points the true lesson. The man is a fool not because of his love of pleasure, but because he thinks that his accumulation of wealth will enable him to control the future. The true foolishness is the illusion of absolute security through property which death destroys. True security, true treasure, is one's present relation to God, and this is absolute because death cannot destroy it.

6. interpreting the times, Luke 12:49-56

What is this "fire"? Is it judgment, the fire of God's love, the fire of the emerging kingdom of God that calls men to repent and perhaps even divides up old loyalties? All these are suggested. "Baptism" here, as in Mark 10:38-39, suggests that the "fire" cannot fully do its work until the suffering and death of the Messiah. There is little reason to be sure that this prediction of the death is a later addition. Jesus by this time has enough evidence to see what the outcome of his message is likely to be.

7. sin, disaster, and repentance, Luke 13:1-5

The problem behind this story is whether or not calamities are caused by sin. Generally, the Jew believed that they were. Some people refer to an incident in which Pilate killed some Jews while they were making their sacrifices. In verse 4 Jesus offers another example of a disaster, and cuts across the traditional explanation. Calamity, he seems to say, cannot be traced directly to sin; but sin is tragically serious, and men must repent, for disaster of perhaps a deeper kind will be their lot if they do not.

8. on discipleship 14:25-35

Luke 14:25-26 suggests that following Jesus must have actually caused the breaking up of family ties. Verse 27 makes the main point of this section, that the life of discipleship is a costly and demanding effort. The two little parables that follow do not quite make the same point. Count the cost, is the meaning of the first;

estimate your foe realistically, is the meaning of the second. Verse 33 explains verse 27 well enough, but the parables stand: vivid, clear, but a little irrelevant to the point. The disciples in verses 34-35 are compared to salt, the means of preserving food. Compare this with the comment on Matthew 5:13, page 29 above.

9. Lazarus and the rich man, Luke 16:19-31

There are a number of themes in this story. It points, in Luke 16:19-26 to the future life as a reversal of the values of this life (see comment on Luke 13:30, above, and also 16:15). It is an expansion of the idea in 16:9 of using money unselfishly (to make friends for yourself). The rich man is condemned not because he is evil or because he is wealthy, but because he ignored Lazarus' need. Verses 27-31 suggest a contrast between Jesus and the Jews (as in 13:20-30); some have thought that this reflects an early church struggle with orthodox Judaism, but it can be more easily understood as Jesus' own criticism of the wealth and worldliness of the Sadducees of his own day.

The word Hades in Luke 16:23 refers to the Hebrew idea of Sheol. In early Jewish thought, this was a place of abode for all the dead where only a bare and shadowy existence went on. When the idea of the final resurrection and judgment came into Jewish thought, Sheol was the waiting place for the disembodied spirits before the last day. In Sheol, some distinctions were worked out, so that even before the final judgment, part of Sheol was like Paradise, and part was like Gehenna, the place of ultimate judgment. Such is the background of this story, and it is an interesting insight into the state of Jewish thought at this time concerning eternal life and final judgment.

10. the coming of the Son of man, Luke 17:22-37

There are two points of interest in the early part of this chapter, prior to the discourse on the Son of man. In 17:7-10, Jesus strikes out against a religious life that is based on rewards given for services performed. God does not reward our virtue; he is gracious to sinners, for we are unworthy even when we have done our best (verse 10). Verses 20-21 are a kind of preface to the discourse to follow: popular guesses about the coming of the kingdom are futile, Jesus argues, for the kingdom is now in the midst of men (verse 21). The saying suggests the present reality of the kingdom, here and now. The astonishing thing is that Jesus seems to say that it is even in the midst of the Pharisees.

In the discourse itself (Luke 17:22-37), Jesus anticipates the early church's perplexity over the nonappearance of the supernatural Son of man, the divine being who will come and usher in the final days at the end of history. This coming, Jesus says, will be sudden and unexpected. In verse 25, Jesus points to his own death, and comes close to identifying himself with the Son of man to whom he refers. The point of the references to Noah and to Lot is not only that the "coming" will be in the midst of normal human activities, but also that there will be a disaster connected with it, like the flood and the fire in the Old Testament stories. This disaster is doubtless intended by Luke to be the death of Christ itself. From verses 31 on, advice is given on how to respond to this catastrophic event: one must be prepared to respond immediately and not look back (for the story of Lot's wife, see Genesis 19:26). Verses 34-37 portray the judgment of the Son of man, a judgment involving destruction. The little proverb in verse 37 should doubtless refer to vultures (this is the reading in the RSV footnote), to make clearer the image of a bird preparing to devour a dead body.

This discourse as a whole reflects the belief of the early church, and surely of Jesus as well, that the end of the world, with the judgment of the Son of man, would speedily come. This did not in fact happen, and this chronological error must be noted. Yet the terrible reality of God's judgment is not thereby made irrelevant. Perhaps the church should have interpreted the resurrection or the gift of the Holy Spirit as the "coming" here referred to; in any case, Christ today "comes" to both the church and the world, as a judge as well as a comforter. The fact that the church expected a coming that did not visibly take place should not blind us to the true meaning of the Gospel as containing the picture of God, always "coming" to us in Christ.

11. some of Luke's characteristic parables

a. the great supper, Luke 14:15-24

Matthew 22:1-10 has a version of this, but it is much more allegorical than Luke's version. Verse 15 gives the excuse for the parable: perhaps Jesus is suggesting that an emotional love for the kingdom of God, as suggested in the exclamation, may not be adequate. A man plans a banquet and invites his friends. They excuse themselves, more or less plausibly. Verses 21-22 may be an allegory, suggesting that if the Jews refuse the kingdom of God, then the others will be invited. There is still room, and so another invitation is offered, this time to those outside the city, that is, to the non-Jew. In verse 24, the banquet is identified with the messianic banquet in the completed kingdom of God. The point of the parable is the contrast between the pious Jew who excused himself, the lowly Jew outside the law, and the Gentile.

b. the three parables of chapter 15: the lost sheep and the lost coin (verses 1-10), and the lost son (11-32)

This magnificent chapter must be seen as a whole. First, notice the question to which the three parables are an answer: Why, the Pharisees murmur, does Jesus consort with sinners? (See Jesus' answer to the same question in Luke 5:29-32.) It is a question of procedure, of ethics. The "answer," however, in the parable is not a piece of self-defense, but a pointer to the character of God. And the meaning of all three parables can be simply put: God takes the initiative and seeks the lost and the sinful, and rejoices when the sinner returns to him. So Jesus' "answer" to the Pharisees is this: Why do I seek the sinner? Because my Father's nature is to seek out those who are lost, and to rejoice in their return. As my Father acts, so do I.

In Luke 15:1-10, then, the two points are made: the shepherd leaves the ninety-nine sheep to seek out the lost one, and rejoices when it is found; the woman drops everything else to seek out the one lost coin (the coin mentioned is probably a Greek drachma, literally worth sixteen cents, but in actual purchasing power many times more than that), and rejoices with her friends when it is found.

The more elaborate details of verses 11-24 should not obscure the fact that the same double point is being made. Note verse 17: "when he came to himself." This does not mean that man has a prior or central role in salvation; but that God's gift of forgiveness can be received only by one who is in need, who knows how to ask the question for which it is the answer. In verses 18-19 the son rehearses the confession he will make to his father. But the father did not simply wait at home for the son, he came down the road to meet him. Before the son can complete his confession, asking for justice and a chance for a fresh beginning, the father greets him with compassion and love. And they rejoice together.

The parallel between the three stories is over, but there is still the curious story of the elder brother (Luke 15:25-32). Now on the human level, we should probably want to feel a good deal of sympathy with him. He'd had extra work to do since his younger brother left, and there is a suggestion that his father had not been grateful. But this parable is not a study in proper family discipline, and as such, it is rather poor advice. We must take the story of the elder brother as a kind of epilogue, tying the central message of the chapter to the setting of verses 1-2. This is a parable spoken in response to a taunt from the Pharisees, and the elder brother (particularly in the rather unlovely protest: "I never disobeyed your command") is probably intended to stand for the Pharisee. The father's response to the brother is in part a rebuke for his unforgiving self-righteousness, just as Jesus' rebuke to the Pharisees tended to be. The father expects even the elder son to rejoice at the prodigal's return; God expects all men (even the Pharisees) to rejoice at Jesus' mission to the lost.

There is a good deal of the central message of the Gospel here; God's gracious and forgiving love is powerfully described. But the whole Gospel is not here, and we must not expect any one parable to contain that; what is not here is what no parable can portray, what only the cross can show—the cost of this love as shown in the death of the Son.

c. the unjust steward, Luke 16:1-13

This is a fascinating example of a parable which is not to be taken as an example by the Christian. The manager of an estate had been careless and was called to account by his master. He became afraid, and persuaded some of those who owed produce to his master to falsify (to their own benefit) their records, so that if the steward should be fired, he would have some who were obligated to him. "The master" in Luke 16:8 has been taken by the RSV translators to mean the master in the parable. He is commending not the dishonesty but the prudence of the man; and verse 9 follows as Jesus' interpretation: in your use of money, he says, be prudent and unselfish ("make friends for yourselves," that is, by giving generously to others, verse 9); for you cannot take it with you, and God is your final treasure in any case. But "master" in verse 8 might mean Jesus; in this case we have the possibility of an added interpretation, for he is then saying something like this: take a lesson from the calculating shrewdness of the men of the world. Be as clever in dealing with the things of God as they are in dealing with the things of this world. He might then be pointing to the very modern contrast which exists in the clever businessman who is very naive or foolish in religious matters.

In verses 10-12 Luke contributes a series of sayings about money so that the parable cannot be misunderstood. Be careful and honest in money matters; and remember, only God—not possessions—can be served.

d. the Pharisee and the publican, Luke 18:9-14

Here is another parable as an example. Not all Pharisees were like this one, but there is evidence that his attitude was not uncommon. The setting is in the temple in Jerusalem. The Pharisee first describes what he does not do; he then mentions what he does do beyond what is required. Fasts were not required by the law; nor were tithes of personal income (which is what is referred to here). The tax collector isolates himself from the rest of the worshipers and confesses his unworthiness. This is a story both about true and false prayer, and about true and false character. Two elements in Phariseeism are underlined here: proud criticism of others and proud congratulation of self. Jesus' teaching as a whole strikes out heavily against these traits in religious man.

V. Matthew and Luke on the Final Days in Jesus' Ministry

Matthew 19—28:20 and Luke 18:15—24:53
(Compare Mark 10—16:8)

In this final section, Matthew and Luke follow Mark's order of events with considerable care, and the reader may wish to make use of the references to Mark's gospel as he proceeds.

1. the trip to Jerusalem, Matthew 19—20 and Luke 18:15—19:27 (compare Mark 10)

When Matthew deals with Jesus' teaching on divorce, he modifies the unconditional prohibition of divorce as found in Mark. Notice Matthew 19:9, the phrase "except for unchastity," which Matthew adds to Jesus' words from Mark. In the story of the rich young man, both Matthew and Luke leave out the touching comment in Mark that Jesus looked on the young man and loved him, after he had claimed obedience to the basic commandments. His discipleship needed one further thing, that he sell all his goods and give the proceeds to the poor. Full obedience for this man meant giving up his wealth, and in face of this demand he turned away sadly. With a touch of humorous exaggeration, Jesus draws a conclusion from this incident. The disciples, though not themselves rich, wonder if any man can be saved. Jesus answers directly: no, not by themselves or on their own merits. God alone can save man, He alone grants his kingdom. Jesus goes on to describe this kingdom as a future blessedness. Even though a man has given up everything to be a disciple, his reward will be beyond his imagining, and human standards of value and worth will be radically overturned.

a. the parable of the laborers in the vineyard, Matthew 20:1-16

This is of course a very poor lesson in labor-management relations, and is not meant to be such. "Vineyard" is a familiar symbol in the Old Testament for Israel (see Isaiah 5:7); and therefore this can be seen as a study in God's justice and freedom in offering the kingdom to whomever he wishes. Verse 15 is the actual point: the kingdom is a gift of grace, not given according to merit or virtue, as the Pharisees and the elder brother in Luke 15 supposed.

In Matthew 20:17-19 (and in Luke 18:31-34) Jesus and his disciples set out for the capital city, and he tells them for the third time what his fate is to be. A prediction of the resurrection is found in both accounts, but the dispersal of the disciples at the time of the arrest, and the element of surprise when the account of the resurrection is received later on, both suggest that these are words which the evangelists place on Jesus' lips at this point. In Matthew 20:20-28, the mother of James and John requests a special place in the kingdom for her sons. Jesus refuses this silly request rather gently, and then deals with the apparently self-righteous anger of the disciples at the request itself. True power is not a kingly power, but lowliness, suffering, and death. The career of the Son of man is to be a model for the career of those who obey him. (Compare Luke 22:24-27.) The blindness of the disciples who do not see this yet, is then contrasted with the story of the blind man (two in Matthew) who is made to see by Jesus (Matthew 20:29-34 and Luke 18:35-43; compare Mark 10:46-52).

b. Zacchaeus, Luke 19:1-10

This may be another version of the call of Levi (Mark 2:13-17 and Luke 5:27-32). Zacchaeus is described as a sort of supervisor of the tax collection in the area, a position that ostracized him from his fellow Jews. He is drawn to Jesus because of Jesus' reputation as a friend of such as he. Jesus calls his name (Luke does not bother to explain how Jesus knew it) and indicates that he wishes to stay at his house. This act of acceptance was the decisive turning-point for Zacchaeus. The bystanders murmur their disapproval in verse 7; Zacchaeus makes a response to Jesus' act of acceptance, and Jesus' words in verse 9 are apparently his answer to the crowd's criticism. Zacchaeus has shown himself to be a true Jew by his response, in spite of his ostracism by his fellow Jews. The story ends, as so often in Luke, with an emphasis on the special value in the kingdom of God of the lost, outcast and rejected.

c. the parable of the talents, Luke 19:11-27 and Matthew 25:14-30

A "talent" was equivalent to about $1000, and our modern use of the word to mean a special aptitude or gift is probably derived from this story. Matthew preserves a fairly simple version of the story. It is not primarily a defense of capitalism or banking, but a warning to the Jews not to be content with their tradition and past, but to develop and use it creatively. It could also be advice to a Christian disciple to make use of what he has, lest even what little (faith) he has to be taken away.

Luke adds a number of details. The man has become a nobleman, who leaves to receive some sort of royal power over his subjects. Some local citizens oppose this, and send a delegation away to complain. On his return, invested with the royal power in spite of the objections, the nobleman rewards the faithful with grants of political power, rebukes the timid ones, and gives an order that the citizens who objected to his appointment be put to death. Thus Luke adds an allegorical meaning beyond what Matthew intended. The nobleman going away to become a king points to the death of Christ, and his return is the second coming. In the interim, the disciples are exhorted to be faithful, for there will be rewards and punishments at the time of the last judgment. Those who hate him and oppose the "appointment" are presumably the Jews. Both versions make the same point: warning to the Jews, and advice to the disciples to be faithful and obedient so that eternal life may be granted (this is the meaning of the phrase "joy of your master" in Matthew 25:21, 23).

2. events and teaching in Jerusalem, Matthew 21:1—25:46, and Luke 19:28—21:38 (compare Mark 11-13)

A very brief outline of these decisive events will be given, before we proceed to deal with the death and resurrection in more detail.

a. the entry into the city, Matthew 21:1-9 and Luke 19:28-38

This entry takes place amidst considerable tension; the crowd not understanding what is going on, the disciples themselves half bewildered, the authorities preparing to strike, and Jesus alone clearly aware of what the future is to be. Matthew makes explicit the messianic character of the entry, by quoting the passage from Zechariah 9:9. Jesus intends this as a symbolic gesture, clear to those who have eyes to see, meaningless to the rest. Here, as elsewhere, he acts out, rather than explicitly describes, his lowly messiahship. Note that Matthew, in his zeal to work out a literal fulfillment of the prophecy, misreads the Old Testament prophecy, and has Jesus in the awkward situation of riding on two animals at once.

b. the cleansing of the temple and the cursing of the fig tree, Matthew 21:10-22 and Luke 19:45-48

Matthew records both these events, and weaves them together; Luke, perhaps embarrassed by the rather unattractive picture of Jesus cursing a tree for not bearing fruit at a time when the fruit was not supposed to grow, drops it. The cleansing is not merely the act of a reformer of piety, but a fulfillment of some Old Testament passages about the messianic age (Isaiah 56:7 and Jeremiah 7:11). Luke radically shortens this story. It is probable that originally the story of the tree was a parable in which Jesus compared Israel to a barren fig tree, and in the process of transmission it became transformed from a parable to a narrative of an actual event.

c. teaching and parables in Jerusalem, Matthew 21:23—24:51 (and 25:31-46) and Luke 20:1—21:36 (compare Mark 11:27—13:37)

1. a question on authority, Matthew 21:23-27 and Luke 20:1-8

Jesus replies to a baited question with a counter-question. If the priests and elders denied John's authority, they would offend the people; if they affirmed it, they would be obliged to affirm Jesus' authority as well.

2. the parable of the two sons, Matthew 21:28-32

The point is in Matthew 21:31; verse 32 seems a rather irrelevant addition, designed to relate this passage to the previous one. Jesus' reply to his questioners could hardly have been more offensive.

3. the wicked tenants, Matthew 21:33-46 and Luke 20:9-19

Two accusations are concealed in this parable or, more accurately, allegory; the Pharisees and priests are accused in advance of murder; and God will reject the Jews because of this criminal act. Israel is the vineyard, God is the owner, the Jews are the tenants, the servants are the prophets, and the son is Jesus himself.

4. the question of paying the poll tax, Matthew 22:15-22 and Luke 20:20-26

Again the question is designed to compromise Jesus; a clear "yes" would have a bad popular effect, and a "no" would portray him as seditious. Just what is Jesus' answer here, and what are the implications of it for a political ethic? What about Acts 5:29 alongside this?

5. on the resurrection, Matthew 22:23-33 and Luke 20:27-40

Jesus doesn't really answer the question put to him, except to suggest that life in the world to come will be of a different order than life here. The real intent of the passage is to base the Christian hope for resurrection on God, and not on anything inherently immortal in man.

6. the great commandment, Matthew 22:34-40 and Luke 10:25-28

A serious question from a Jew this time, not an attempt to trap Jesus. And Jesus answers it directly.

Following this is a question about the Messiah's descent from David (which Jesus seems to deny, Matthew 22:41-46 and Luke 20:41-44); and a long criticism of the Pharisees, Matthew 23: 1-36 and, more briefly, in Luke 20:45-47.

7. the apocalyptic discourse, Matthew 24:1-51 and Luke 21:5-36

For a number of reasons, most observers agree that this material is from a variety of sources; there may be some authentic teaching of Jesus here, but there is also some material that the church used to warn the Christians to flee from Jerusalem at the time of the Roman attack in A.D. 70. Instead of answering the question about the fall of the temple, Jesus speaks of events leading up to the final catastrophic end of all things. There is a great deal of Old Testament quotation and paraphrase here, and as a whole it is too unoriginal to be taken in any full sense as authentic words of Jesus. Matthew (verses 37-51) concludes this discourse with advice on the need for watchfulness, though the reference in the conclusion may be to the coming crisis in Jesus' own ministry and not to the end of the world. If the reader keeps in mind these two references:

to the coming crisis in Jesus' own ministry and to the persecution of the church in Matthew and Luke's time; and if he further understands that apocalyptic thinking about the future of the world is a perennial temptation in time of political or cultural despair (science fiction today is a sort of secular apocalyptic), these passages will speak movingly of the power of God even in the darkest days.

8. the last judgment, Matthew 25:31-46

The "Son of man" coming at the end of time as judge is a messianic figure (he is also called a king), but Jesus does not here identify himself with that figure. The motif is one we have already become familiar with in Matthew and Luke: humble and self-effacing service is a mark of obedience to the Messiah and his kingdom, even if one is unaware that one's service is in fact obedience to Christ. The touch of surprise in verse 38 is interesting. It may be that it is not general benevolence to all men that is described here, but rather service to the disciples of Jesus. "My brethren" in verse 40 may mean this, and Matthew 12:48-49 seems to stand as evidence for such an interpretation.

In any case, the decision against the Messiah has already been made by the Jews. The humble and lowly and sinful have obeyed; the religious leaders have rejected him. What follows is in a way both epilogue and climax. The Passion story itself works out the implications both of Jesus' rejection and the meaning of accepting and following him.

3. the Passion and resurrection narratives, Matthew 26—28 and Luke 22—24 (compare Mark 14—16:8)

Matthew and Luke follow Mark fairly closely in their accounts of the events leading up to the last supper: the plot, Judas' betrayal, the preparation of the last supper, and the prediction of the betrayal (Matthew 26:1-19 and Luke 22:1-13, compare Mark

14:17-25). But Matthew alone includes here the story of the anointing at Bethany (26:6-13). This needs some comment. In verse 11 Jesus is saying that of course service to the poor is always required, but in this particular case the woman has performed an act that makes practical criticism irrelevant. But what had she done? She had "anointed" Jesus. What makes the act worthy of such praise? Two meanings are contained in the woman's act: it is first a confession that Jesus is the Messiah, the "anointed" one. She is also pointing to his death and burial, for the dead are anointed as well. And so the woman has seen something that the disciples themselves had not seen up until now: that Jesus' messiahship is a suffering one, and that it will lead to death.

a. the last supper, Matthew 26:17-29 and Luke 22:14-38 (compare Mark 14:17-25)

Matthew and Luke, like Mark, describe this day as the one before Passover, interpreting the trial and the death as falling on Passover itself. Thus Jesus is seen as bearing a new covenant, related to the old covenant given through Moses. John puts the crucifixion on the day before Passover, the day when the lambs are slaughtered for the feast. Matthew is quite close to Mark in this story, but Luke has some significant variations: the cup comes before the bread and is not related to the new covenant. He also stresses, in verses 16 and 18, the element of anticipation in a way that reminds us of I Corinthians 11:26. Luke may have an independent source for this event. The bread is broken, and the wine is released, given, poured out. These are the central gestures in this story and are the clues to what was being enacted by Jesus before his perhaps uncomprehending disciples. The broken bread points forward to the actual breaking of the body on the cross the following day. What of the pouring of the wine? The blood, remember, is the source of life in Jewish psychology, and so it is not death that is involved in the shedding of blood, but the new gift of new life. Thus both death and resurrection seem to be anticipated in Jesus' words and gestures.

When the Christian church celebrates the central act of its worship—whether it calls it Mass, Eucharist, Holy Communion, or Lord's Supper—it points back not only to these events in the upper room, but to the whole drama of God's redemptive action that Jesus is symbolizing in his words and gestures.

b. Gethsemane, Matthew 26:36-46 and Luke 22:40-46 (compare Mark 14:32-42)

Matthew follows Mark almost word for word, but Luke has made the scene if anything more vivid and powerful. The threefold falling asleep of the disciples is cut; the vision of an angel is added, and the anguish is deepened. The reader should note just what is being said here: a few hours before his death, Jesus prayed that it not come to pass. He in effect rebelled against God. Only after his rebellion did he give himself into God's hands.

In the story of the arrest that immediately follows, Matthew has added a saying about Jesus' power to call into his service an army of angels, and Luke has added a rather perfunctory miracle of healing the ear of the slave that one of the disciples cut off in anger. Note that Luke has not included the humiliating fact of the disciples' flight after the arrest (Matthew 26:56).

c. the trials, ecclesiastical and civil, Matthew 26:57—27:31, Luke 22:54—23:25 (compare Mark 14:53—15:15)

The trial before Caiaphas (Matthew names him) was probably not an official trial so much as a preliminary hearing to get evidence to present to Pilate. There were strict rules of evidence, and witnesses were unable to agree (each witness had to be examined individually, and there had to be clear agreement). So they began instead to question Jesus himself, to see if he would claim to be Messiah in order that they might present him to Pilate as a royal pretender to the Jewish throne (of Herod). Note that Matthew (26:64) and Luke (22:67-70) slightly modify Mark's version of Jesus' response to the high priest's question about his status as Messiah. In Matthew, Jesus replies "You have said so"; and in Luke, "You say that I am." Note also that Matthew and Luke clarify what is happening in Mark 14:65, by adding the taunting question, "Who is it that struck you?" This is a little game; if you are a prophet, they say, put on this blindfold and guess which one of us is hitting you.

Matthew 27:3-10 gives an account of Judas' repentance and suicide. Compare with this the brief account in Acts 1:18-19. The actual repentance and remorse is plausible, but it looks as if the rest of the passage (verses 5-10) is built up around the quotation from the Old Testament.

Matthew is closer to Mark in his record of the trial before Pilate than Luke, but even in Matthew we have a little more emphasis on Pilate's conviction of Jesus' innocence than in Mark (Matthew 27:23-25). Luke adds to Mark the Jewish complaints at the beginning of the hearing (Luke 23:2-5), several protests by Pilate of his conviction of Jesus' innocence, and Pilate's attempt to avoid responsibility of referring Jesus to Herod, the tetrarch, who is apparently in Jerusalem at the time (Luke 23:6-16). But Herod finds no crime in him, and sends him back to Pilate who again declares for his innocence.

Pilate's role in all this is difficult to assess. It may well be that the church at the end of the first century, living under Roman rule and permission, is anxious to underline the Jewish responsibility and to minimize the Roman part. But Jesus is, after all, crucified, and this is a Roman method, and the charge posted on the cross was a political not a religious one. Pilate's superior, the emperor Tiberius, was known to be merciless to suspected traitors, but he was also careful that prisoners not be mistreated. Apparently Pilate, even though he saw the motives of the high priests clearly, feared an uprising even more, and gave orders that the prisoner be condemned and crucified.

Luke adds a moving scene on the way to Calvary, 23:26-31. Pity, Jesus says, is not what is required now. The women of Jerusalem have more reason for tears than they realize, he says. The Jewish rejection of the Messiah may be the greater reason for grief, and Luke's readers will certainly have thought of the actual fall of Jerusalem and the temple in A.D. 70.

d. crucifixion, death, and burial, Matthew 27:32-66 and 28:11-15; Luke 23:32-56 (compare Mark 15:22-47)

Matthew and Luke preserve the same form and simplicity in their accounts that is found in Mark. But some of the differences should be noted. Luke has translated the Aramaic Golgotha into "the Skull." In verses 34-35 Luke adds a saying of Jesus on the cross that is unique to him. Whom is Jesus forgiving here? The Jews or the Romans or both? Matthew adds, in verse 36, a saying about the soldiers keeping watch over the body, perhaps to prepare the reader for verses 62-66. He also adds the phrase "Son of God" in verse 40, recalling that the high priest had used this phrase in his question at the trial (26:63).

Luke, in verses 39-43, adds some sayings of the two criminals crucified with Jesus. The one who asks Jesus to remember him when he comes into his kingly power receives an even greater promise. "Today you will be with me in Paradise." "Paradise" is a Persian word, and it reminds us that in Jewish thought was emerging—along with the older idea that the spirits of the dead would dwell in Sheol until the final resurrection and judgment—this newer idea that the righteous went immediately to their reward after death.

Luke does not record the terrible cry of dereliction from the cross (Matthew 27:46), including in its place a quotation from Psalm 31:5. We cannot hope to penetrate its meaning adequately, though it is surely right to see in it something of the cost to Christ, and even to God, of the bearing of human sin. In this cry, we catch something of the depth to which God stoops in Christ; He comes fully into our humanity, our sin, and, perhaps, even into our despair. The drink of vinegar (Matthew 27:48) may be an act of mercy, or it may be another form of abuse (see Psalm 69:21).

In Mark, the centurion expresses admiration at Jesus' courage in the face of death. In Luke, he declares Jesus' innocence, verse 47, and in Matthew, verse 54, both the centurion and some bystanders are filled with awe. Note that Luke, verse 49, suggests (in the phrase "all his acquaintances") that the disciples had not all fled at the time of the arrest.

Matthew 27:62-66 and 28:11-15 are pieces of legendary material added by Matthew. They seem highly improbable. They were possibly added by early Christians to repudiate the charge that Jesus' body was merely stolen from the tomb by the disciples. It is unlikely that the high priests would have taken Jesus' prediction of his resurrection seriously, even if they had known about it: after all, the disciples themselves were surprised by it. And it is further unlikely that Pilate would have consented to give a guard to the Jews; he has not been portrayed as exactly friendly to them. However suspicious we may be of the sources of this material, it does at least show that there was an empty tomb that needed explaining.

e. the resurrection, Matthew 28:1-20 and Luke 24:1-53

1. the empty tomb, Matthew 28:1-10 and Luke 24:1-11

Matthew and Luke both take over Mark 16:1-8, and make some significant additions. In Matthew, the women do not come to anoint the body, as in Mark, presumably because of the presence of the guard. Matthew adds the touches of supernatural wonder in verses 2-4 and the note about the helplessness of the guards. After the angle's words in Matthew, the women depart in fear and joy to tell the disciples, and Jesus meets them. Note their response: they both worship and touch him, an indication that Matthew intends us to understand that this is no hallucination or vision. Jesus tells the women that he will appear again in Galilee to the disciples.

In Luke, Jesus does not appear to the women, and the message they rush off to report is merely the words of the two angels. The curious fact, in verse 11, that the disciples did not believe may be contradicted by verse 24. Remember that in Mark and Matthew, the disciples had all gone home to Galilee by the time of the arrest; only in Luke 23:49 are they said still to be in Jerusalem. The contrast between the silence of the women in Mark 16:8 and the eagerness to report in Matthew and Luke is interesting.

2. the command to baptize, Matthew 28:16-20

Here the promise of verse 10 is fulfilled. These verses probably reflect the early church's interpretation more than Jesus' actual words, but they make a striking climax to the gospel. The miraculous is set aside, for it is not the final word. The final word is obedience and service on behalf of the risen Lord. No part of the Bible has given Christians such a sense of the world-wide church. Note that this saying, like the ten commandments, and like the Sermon on the Mount, is given from a mountain. Some of the disciples believed, and some did not (Jesus himself had said that a resurrection would not convince everyone, Luke 16:31). He speaks of his authority and of their obedience. He promises them his presence, until the very end of human history itself, when all people will inherit the kingdom of God and see him face to face.

3. resurrection appearances in Luke 24:13-53

a. the Emmaus road, 24:13-35

These two were not apparently among the original disciples, but of that other group who heard the women's story of the tomb and disbelieved it (in verses 9, 10, 11). They are on their way home from Jerusalem, and the risen Lord draws near. They do not recognize him, and Luke suggests it is because their understanding has been dulled by God. Compare Mary's confusion of the risen Christ with the gardener in John 20:14-16. The disciples describe what they had hoped for in Jesus in terms that are very similar to the early sermons of Peter in Acts 2. The cross has left them desolate, and the story of the empty tomb has not lifted their gloom. Verse 26 suggests that Christ has already entered into his glory, yet it is clearly a glory that is not overpoweringly self-evident. It has to be discerned. Their hearts burn, they later say, when Jesus expounds the bibical story, but they do not really see who he is until they break bread together. This meal seems similar to the last supper, and may have been thought of by Luke as a sort of early Lord's Supper. When they recognized him, he disappeared. They returned to Jerusalem to tell the original disciples; in the meantime, Jesus had appeared to Peter.

This story is in many ways the most vivid insight into the early church's understanding of the resurrection of Christ that we have. It was clearly understood as an historical event, but it was obviously something more. Three different stages in the disciples' understanding can be noticed: they see and listen to him; they discern who he is; and they make an appropriate response—returning to the city with the message, "The Lord has risen indeed." The resurrection cannot here be less than event (physical, it is sometimes called); but it must be something more. Discernment of its meaning in the context of the whole biblical story must come; this is the significance of the exposition of the Bible along the way. And finally, before it can be truly an experience of the risen Lord, the disciple must make a response of obedience. Thomas, remember, had first to see and to touch; only then did he find it possible to say, "My Lord and my God!" (John 20:28).

b. Christ's appearance in Jerusalem, Luke 24:36-49

The story of the Emmaus road is not explicit as to the form of the risen Christ. This story of the appearance to the disciples in Jerusalem in the midst of the report of the two from Emmaus, contains an insistence that Jesus' risen form was physical. He invites them to touch him; he eats fish in their presence. There is a slight difference of emphasis between this and the earlier story. There Jesus is seen, but he is not discerned or fully understood all at once. Here the appearance is interpreted as more self-evident, in spite of the wonderful phrase in verse 41: "they still disbelieved for joy."

The final words are quiet and moving. The supernatural and miraculous atmosphere has lifted, and the final emphasis is on the work to be done. Christ interprets his meaning; he gives his disciples their commission, and bids them wait for the gift of the Holy Spirit, promised in the prophecy of Joel 2:28-29 and given at Pentecost in Acts 2 (but see John 20:22).

c. the ascension, Luke 24:50-53

By comparing the Revised Standard Version and the King James here, you will notice that the statement that Jesus "was . . . carried up into heaven" (verse 51, KJV) is not found in the best manuscripts, and is therefore not included in the translation. Nevertheless, this is the story of the ascension that Luke interprets more fully in Acts 1:6-11. Apparently, by the time he began on the second volume of his work he had come into possession of new material indicating that Jesus' appearances lasted for forty days. Here in the gospel, the ascension takes place on the day of the resurrection. We need not worry overmuch about the actual meaning of the ascension. The incident seems played down here in any case; Jesus' work is done, and the disciples know who he is. His presence is no longer needed as before, and it is withdrawn. The response of the disciples is the only appropriate one: they praise God with joy and gratitude, and prepare to serve him in the world.

The true "problem" at the end here is not the problem of ascension, it is the problem of service and obedience. Since all these things have happened, what is to be done? The second volume of Luke's book (The Acts of the Apostles) begins the answer to that, and the history of the church up to today continues it.

PART TWO

MARK

Introduction

In the winter of A.D. 64-65 a great fire broke out in Rome, and the emperor Nero looked around for someone to blame. He decided to accuse the Christians who were generally unpopular and were thought to harbor revolutionary ideas. A reign of terror followed; Peter and Paul were probably among the victims.

Shortly after this a little book appeared in Rome bearing the title "The Gospel of Jesus Christ." It was what we know as Mark's gospel, and we can guess at the motives which led to its appearance. Christians under persecution needed to be reminded of their Master and of the sufferings he had undergone. Especially now that the older generation who had known him was dying off, the remembered facts about Jesus needed to be set down.

Let us look at the historical situation at the time. Palestine is under Roman military and civil occupation. A priestly aristocracy (the Sadducees) is chiefly concerned to maintain its own privileged position under the Romans. The religious leaders (the Pharisees) have largely ceased to give an effective lead, and have become more and more absorbed in pious practices at the cost of the "weightier matters of the Law." The common people are neglected and depressed. Political agitators and religious fanatics are preaching violence. There are wild hopes in the air of revolution or of an approaching miraculous deliverance associated with the name of the coming Messiah or Christ. Forty years later, indeed, these pressures were to erupt into a disastrous war which would finish the Jewish state. At the time of which we are speaking, they are brewing.

Into this scene Jesus entered. His answers to the question about the tax to Caesar (12:17) probably bothered the nationalists. His act of clearing the temple of money-changers upset the priests. His attitude to the Sabbath laws disturbed the pious. Very few understood his association with the people outside the Jewish law—the publicans and sinners. Since he offended nearly everyone, it is not surprising that the Jewish authorities were able to agree to have him put out of the way.

As you read through The Gospel according to Mark, you will note that it is in the form of a series of episodes, loosely strung together. An episode may be told with a good deal of picturesque detail, but then the author is likely to pass on to something else quite abruptly with only a bare summary to show the interconnection. There is little in Mark that can be called continuous biographical narrative.

There is one exception. In Chapters 14 and 15—the so-called Passion story—we find a continuous narrative, telling in detail how Jesus was seized by his enemies, tried and put to death. At first reading this Passion narrative seems simply to be the story of a good man, denied and deserted by his followers, trapped by religious leaders, condemned by a timid judge, and put to an ignominious death.

A second glance, however, at these critical chapters reveals that there is something more here than a tale of martyrdom. There is a mysterious undercurrent. For example, after the homely details of the preparation of the last supper with the disciples, we read the strange words, "this is my body," "this is my blood . . . poured out for many." The death to come is said to be like a sacrifice, re-establishing a new set of relations between God and man. Again, in the garden of Gethsemane, Jesus says that God wants this execution to take place. Before the high priest, Jesus apparently declares that he is the Messiah, the Son of God, and adds something about the Son of man returning to the right hand of God. Finally, at the end, the "curtain of the temple was torn in two, from top to bottom." This curtain was what hid the presence of God from the people in the Jewish worship, and Mark is apparently suggesting that in the death of Jesus there was something that removed the curtain and made God more accessible. Something deeper and more mysterious is going on, something to do with God's access to men and the deepest issues of human destiny.

Over and over again we hear of a "secret" that must be kept until the right time comes, a secret that seems to have something to do with God's rule over the world. The mystery of the kingdom of God, Mark calls it. It is also the secret of who Jesus really is. Teacher, prophet, reformer, leader? Yes, but what else? The question is put by Jesus himself to his disciples (8:27) in a scene which is evidently intended to be one of the highlights of the picture. The disciples partly understand and partly do not.

Jesus moves throughout this story almost incognito. He is always something more than appears. But although the actors in the story are barely half aware whom they are dealing with, Mark has already taken his readers into his confidence in the opening verses of the gospel. Here Jesus is contrasted with John the Baptist, here his "secret" is spoken by a divine voice which he alone hears. He is the supernatural Son of God. And soon we stumble upon his works of healing, done with a strange authority. Later we read words, scarcely understood at all by the disciples at the time, about the Son of man having to suffer and die, and be raised again. Who was this man, and what was happening through him? This is *the* question of the gospel, and to it we must now turn.

I. Prologue to Mark's Gospel

1:1-13

1. John the Baptist and his message, 1:1-8

Verse 1 is properly the title of the whole work. The word "Gospel" does not refer to the book itself, or to the words spoken by Jesus. It means the good news of God which is announced through Jesus Christ. Mark speaks of Jesus Christ: Jesus is the Greek form of the Jewish name Joshua; Christ is the Greek equivalent of the Jewish term Messiah, the divine deliverer expected by the Jewish people. At first, Christ was a title; by now it has become part of the proper name.

"Son of God" is perhaps Mark's most significant description of Jesus. It is well to note the decisive places "Son of God" appears in the gospel: here; in the mouths of the demoniacs in 3:11 and 5:7; in the question of the high priest in 14:61; and also in 1:11, 9:7, and (possibly) 13:32. For Mark, Son of God refers to a divine being that appears in human form. Mark takes with full seriousness the reality of the earthly life of Jesus, but for him this lowly man of suffering is of supernatural origin. This origin, we shall see, is concealed from all except those who are prepared to understand. One of the basic questions of this gospel lies precisely here: How can one prepare himself to receive this truth? The question is raised in many forms in the New Testament. As Mark phrases it, it is this: How can one enter the kingdom of God? But when Paul speaks of salvation or redemption, or when John tells of the gift of new and eternal life, it is the same gift of God that is being described. "Son of God" does not refer to Jesus as the

Messiah; Mark has other ways of describing this; it is his way of describing Jesus' utterly unique relationship to God and His purpose.

John the Baptist is portrayed as one of the Old Testament prophets, dressed as they were, preaching a similar message of repentance and forgiveness. The locusts he ate were the insects, not the seeds of the tree. He expresses his humility by declaring himself unfit even to perform the slave's task of untying the sandal of the one who is to come after him.

2. Jesus' baptism, 1:9-11

The baptism that John performed required repentance, yet Jesus submitted himself to this baptism. Did he confess his sin? Mark is not yet aware of this problem, though Matthew 3:14-15 attempts to deal with it. When we try to penetrate behind the imagery, just what event in the career of Jesus is being portrayed? The heavens open: God's access to man is now made direct. A voice from God speaks: Jesus' vocation is defined. (If you look carefully at these words you will see that they are taken from Psalm 2:7 and Isaiah 42:1. Already at the beginning, Jesus' meaning is being defined in terms both of the divine Son of God and of the lowly servant of God.) The Spirit descends: power is given to perform his ministry. This does not mean that because the Spirit descended on Jesus he then became the Son of God. The descent of the Spirit is a sign pointing to the fact that he is already, and has been from the beginning, God's Son.

The "voice" is heard only by Jesus himself. A clear-cut decision has been made about his relation to the kingdom of God.

3. the temptation, 1:12-13

Notice the contrast between the very exalted experience of baptism and this description of loneliness and perhaps even terror. The fuller accounts of this in Matthew 4:1-11 and Luke 4:1-13 help us to round out our picture of the meaning of these verses. God drives Jesus to the wilderness, but it is Satan that tempts him.

II. The Ministry in Galilee

1:14—6:13

1. the first phase, 1:14—3:6

Any divisions of the material are always partly arbitrary. Perhaps the best way is to try to organize the material by means of the geography. This first phase finds Jesus mainly in the towns. After 3:6 he goes into the countryside because of growing hostility toward him.

a. summary statement, 1:14-15

This is a very important passage. The decisive moment for God's action has come. *The whole New Testament can be seen as an expansion of these two verses.*

Mark sets the beginning of Jesus' ministry at the time of John's arrest. The word for "time" here means the right time, the decisive moment. In Galatians 4:4, Paul has a similar idea. To say the time is fulfilled is to say that the ministry of Jesus Christ is part of a divine plan, part of God's whole purpose for the redemption of the world.

"Kingdom of God" does not mean an earthly utopia or a just social order; it is God's sovereignty or rule, breaking in now, and shortly to be fully revealed. It is at hand, very near. It is a gift of a new kind of personal and corporate life that God is giving to man. In some of the parables, the emphasis falls on its being already present: see 4:3-9, 26-29, 30-32. But this is not Mark's main emphasis, as it is, for example, in the Fourth Gospel. Mark's position is that the kingdom is here, yet not quite here, and he maintains this tension throughout. God is in the process of doing a decisive thing for men. Jesus asks: Do you wish to understand and receive it? Two things are necessary: repent and believe in the Gospel. To repent is not merely to be sorry for mistakes, it is to make a radical break with one's present way of life. "Believe" means to give oneself in complete trust and obedience to God who is making himself known in the work of Jesus Christ.

b. the first disciples are called, 1:16-20

The kingdom of God has been announced, and now there is work to be done on its behalf. The Christian faith is not only an individual affair, it also involves a new kind of community. Two groups of two each are summoned first. Notice the "immediately" of verses 18 and 20. Mark likes to use this word, and it gives a note of urgency to his narrative. Perhaps the first readers of the gospel were expected to learn from the immediacy of the response here: no time for excuses. Christ calls, and men follow at once.

It is probable that from verse 16 to the end of this chapter we have a continuous narrative of a single 24-hour period in the early ministry of Jesus.

c. at Capernaum, 1:21-39

1. the demoniac in the synagogue, 1:21-28

The thing that astonishes the hearers is Jesus' direct claim to be speaking for God and his refusal to cite traditional authorities for his teaching, as the scribes did.

A mentally deranged man approaches him, apparently with some fear. Without any elaborate gestures, Jesus cures the man.

Again people are astonished, not that he could quiet a demoniac —many exorcists at this time did that—but that he did it so simply with only a word of command. The convulsions of verse 26 suggest epilepsy. Apparently there is a power in Jesus that some can already discern, and, oddly enough, the poor madman is able to perceive it, though the disciples never fully understood it until after the resurrection.

This is the first of many stories of healing in this gospel. We have to remember that physical evil or disease in biblical times had two possible interpretations. One, that it was a punishment for sin (Job's friends take this position in their argument, and see also John 9:2); another, that the demons visited even good men and took control of them. We must try to understand the meaning of these narratives before we too easily reject them. The healings must be seen as signs of the emerging rule or kingdom of God (see Matthew 12:28), and also as expressions of Jesus' concern for the physical (as well as the spiritual) part of a man. Before we become too certain that things like this cannot happen, we might want to look at more recent claims for spiritual healing. And we ought to add that we make nonsense of the gospel story if we arbitrarily drop out all the healing "miracles." Each one must be studied on its own merits.

2. *Peter's mother-in-law, 1:29-31*

This incident takes place at Peter's home in Capernaum, and the lifelike detail suggests that it comes from the recollection of Peter himself. Notice the woman's response of gratitude after her fever is relieved.

3. *other healings that evening, 1:32-34*

The sun has set, and the Sabbath is technically over, so now devout Jews may bring their sick to Jesus without fear of breaking the law. Again the demons seem to have a special insight into the character of Jesus, and he forbids them to speak.

4. withdrawal and return, 1:35-39

After a day of healing and preaching, Jesus withdraws for prayer. We must be careful in our interpretation of Christ that we do not make improbable or unreal his habit of prayer to the Father. He prayed because he needed to pray.

d. the cure of a leper, 1:40-45

This may not have been a case of what we call leprosy; more likely it was a skin disease like eczema. The phrase "moved with pity" in verse 41 probably read "moved with anger" in the original, and has here been toned down by Mark. What was it that angered Jesus? Not the interruption surely; not even the man's implied doubt of Jesus' willingness to cure him. Perhaps this anger describes Jesus' reaction to the disease itself. Jesus bids the man follow the Jewish laws controlling leprosy: to go directly to the priest so that the cure can be verified, and to be silent about the cure in public. But the man disobeyed, and Jesus is again restricted in his movements.

e. conflicts with the scribes, 2:1—3:6

1. the paralytic and forgiveness, 2:1-12

There is a break of a few days. Jesus returns to Capernaum, where he had been staying, perhaps at Peter's house. Four men bearing another man on a stretcher approach. Unable to make their way through the crowd at the front door, they go up to the roof by an outside stairway. Making an opening in the roof (made of branches and mud), they lower the man into Jesus' presence. Jesus comments on their faith, and pronounces the paralytic's sins forgiven.

We must remember that one of the traditional explanations of disease is that it is caused by sin. In forgiving the sick man, he assumes that man's physical and spiritual needs are all of a piece.

The claim to forgive is what offends the scribes. Only God can forgive, so these words of Jesus are blasphemy to them. Jesus discerns their objections, and in addition to forgiving the man, cures him as well. Now the Messiah was not expected to forgive sins in Jewish thought, so the scribes are not faced with a messianic claim. This is something more serious: a claim to a direct and unique relation to God himself. Two miracles have taken place: a man has been healed, and a man has received the divine pardon through Jesus. Both healing and forgiveness are God's work, so Jesus is acting out indirectly, rather than explicitly declaring, his meaning and status.

"Son of man" in verse 10 is the first occurrence of this important phrase. It comes from Daniel 7:13, where the seer sees a human figure receiving power and glory at God's hands. The title originally, therefore, suggests a supernatural divine figure, and it was not commonly used for the Messiah. Jesus takes this picture of the heavenly man, and fuses with it the conception of the humble and suffering servant from Isaiah 53. The Son of man comes to earth and suffers and dies at the hands of lawless men. This double conception is the clue to the mystery of Jesus' messiahship. Sometimes Mark's use of "Son of man" points to the exalted and heavenly figure (8:38, 14:62), sometimes the humility is emphasized (8:31, 10:45).

2. *the call of Levi, 2:13-14*

The methods of tax collecting in those days gave a good deal of opportunity for graft, and tax collectors as a group were generally disliked. A Jew in this position would have broken the law forbidding physical contact with the Gentile. Levi here has traditionally been identified with Matthew, the author of the first gospel, but one cannot be certain of this.

3. eating with tax collectors and sinners, 2:15-17

"Sinners" refers to all those who fell short of the rigorous Pharisaic interpretation of the law. Some of the scribes belonging to the strict Pharisee party accused the disciples: Why does he eat with such riffraff? Jesus' reply has a note of irony. A physician can do nothing for the sick if he doesn't seek them out to help them. You, he remarks to the Pharisees, are of course righteous men and need no healing. But the Gospel of the kingdom is for sinners, not for those who think they are righteous. There is a hint here, as in the whole of Jesus' profound analysis of self-righteousness, that the man who thinks he is righteous is worse off than the man who admits his need.

Jesus' response in verse 17 has an exact parallel in Paul's great summary of the Gospel in Romans 5:8: "God shows his love for us in that while we were yet sinners Christ died for us."

4. fasting, 2:18-22

John's disciples were a distinct group for some time after their master's arrest and death, and they and the Pharisees both made a practice of fasting, though it was not required by Jewish law. Jesus is asked why his disciples do not do the same. Verse 20 clearly refers to Jesus' death, though no one understands it as such. There is no reason to suspect that this veiled reference to Jesus' death was added later. Jesus already has confronted his opponents in controversy, and soon (in 3:6) we read that a plan to destroy him is being discussed.

5. on the Sabbath, 2:23-28

Here the disciples are accused by the Pharisees of breaking the law prohibiting the reaping of grain on the Sabbath. Jesus responds with an argument based on their own authority, the scriptures. If David could take food on the Sabbath for his hungry men, surely the disciples are entitled to do the same. Human need takes precedence over the law. The final phrase, ". . . the Son of man is lord even of the Sabbath," does not mean that any man is master over the law. It means that Jesus Christ as the Son of man, God's unique messenger, is lord of the Sabbath and its laws. Why? Because with him the messianic age has dawned, and the Sabbath laws may be put aside during this time of joy. This does not mean that disciples, then or now, do not need law for the regulation of their moral lives. Because of our weakness, we shall always need the correction of the law. It does mean, however, that in Jesus Christ we see not a new set of laws but a new kind of divine love. Christ's love is always destructive of even the best human law and goodness; this is why he was so dangerous then, and it is why Christianity is always potentially a revolutionary threat.

6. the man with the withered hand, 3:1-6

Here Jesus himself, and not the disciples as above, is accused of breaking a law which required that only in extreme emergency could acts of healing be performed on the Sabbath. He answers with a direct and unanswerable counterquestion.

After these two clear instances of violation of their traditions, the Pharisees have apparently made up their minds about Jesus (see verse 6). The Herodians mentioned here were a conservative Jewish group that hoped for a restoration of the monarchy of Herod. Here is the first clear warning of tragedy to come; the shadow of the cross is already hanging over these early events.

2. the second phase of the ministry in Galilee, 3:7—6:13

a. summary statement: the crowds by the lake, 3:7-12

In spite of the growing hostility that has forced Jesus to carry on his work outside the towns by the lakeside, a large crowd continues to listen to him.

b. appointment of the twelve, 3:13-19

These verses mark a decisive moment in the ministry and in the history of the Christian church. In this section, we begin with the appointment of the twelve disciples, and close with their mission. The number 12 may well be significant: there were twelve tribes in Israel, and the disciples are to be the beginning of a new Israel, the new people of God, the church. In verse 14, we find the two-fold task of the disciple. For a while at the beginning he was to stay with Jesus, to learn, listen, and understand. But later he was to be sent out to do the same work Jesus was already doing—preaching the Gospel of the kingdom, and healing the broken bodies and minds of men. This has always been the double task of the Christian community, not merely the task of its official leaders. (A fundamental difference between the Protestant and the Roman Catholic can be discerned here: to the question, "Who is the legitimate successor to the disciple?" the Protestant answers: the body of believers, the church. The Roman Catholic answers in terms of the priestly hierarchy.)

Peter is a name that means "the rock." This may refer to his rugged character and appearance, or it may refer to his position as a foundation of the church, an early witness to the resurrection. "Sons of thunder" may have something to do with the volatile tempers of James and John. The meaning of "Cananaean" is probably "Zealot"—a member of an extreme nationalist group of

Pharisees which hoped to drive the Romans from the country by force.

c. charges against Jesus, 3:19-35

Back home, eating with his family and friends, Jesus is still claimed by the crowds. He gives himself so intensely to the needs of the crowd that his family suspects he is out of his mind. "Friends" in verse 21 probably should read "family." Apparently the local Pharisees have called some scribes down from Jerusalem to observe Jesus, and they enter the controversy. Playing on the suspicions of the family, they suggest that Jesus is possessed by the prince of demons, Satan himself. They cannot deny his power to heal, but they suggest that this power is a devilish one, not divine. (Of course, if Jesus is not what he claims to be, the scribes are right. He *is* mad, dangerously deluded, and he has deceived well-meaning people ever since.)

Jesus replies with two brief parables. Satan is in charge of a kingdom of evil. Why should he stir up division within this kingdom, if I am part of it, Jesus asks. Since I am engaged in a battle against the kingdom of evil, I can hardly be on the side of the head of that kingdom. The strong man's house and goods, in the second parable, refer to Satan and his possession of men. Jesus himself is the one who enters and binds the strong man by casting out demons and freeing men from evil and disease.

The passage in verses 28-30 on the unforgivable sin has often caused sensitive people much distress. Jesus makes it clear what that sin is: ascribing to the devil what belongs to God, making evil into a god. Jesus may not be directly accusing his family and the scribes of committing such a sin, but he does suggest that they are close to it. The apparent harshness of this saying must be set alongside verse 28 with its emphasis that all sins, even blasphemy, will be forgiven.

This section concludes in verses 31-35 with a saying about the true family of Jesus. It is hard not to discern here a note of disappointment in Jesus' attitude toward his mother and brothers. Tradition has sometimes tried to explain away this direct reference to Jesus' brothers; some have tried to say that they were half brothers or cousins. But there is no possible escape from the meaning of the word; they are his true brothers, the younger sons of Mary. It is probable that Mark knows nothing of the virgin birth tradition; this story of course neither supports nor denies it.

Whoever is obedient to God's will is the true family of Jesus. If the actual family do not understand him, they are no longer his true family. This must have come home with real comfort to the persecuted church in Mark's day, with its broken families and temptations to recant based on family loyalty.

d. what is a parable, and why is it used?, 4:1-34

This chapter contains several parables, an interpretation of a parable, and some remarks on their significance and use. Several things should be noted on the parable form itself. Jesus did not invent it (it is found in the Old Testament; see II Samuel 12:1-6), but he gave it its highest expression. In essence a parable is a comparison, usually of God or the kingdom of God to some ordinary event or thing. It must be distinguished from allegory in which every detail of the story has symbolic significance. The parable has but one point to make, and the descriptive details are not independently important except as they clarify the single point and the response that is expected.

1. the sower, 4:1-9

This parable can be seen as Jesus' reflection on the progress of his mission in Galilee, its success and failure. The seed is the Gospel of the kingdom; but it is responded to in different ways. Its reception depends on the kind of soil that receives it. In verse 9, a sense of responsibility is impressed on the hearers, as if to say: make sure that your response is like the last one, the good soil bringing forth fruit.

2. the purpose of parables, 4:10-12

Later, when they are alone with Jesus, the disciples ask about the purpose of Jesus' parabolic teaching. Jesus replies that parables are meant to conceal the truth from the unprepared so that they might receive the judgment they deserve, and not repent and be forgiven.

Some observers defend the saying, calling it hard but true. They point to Isaiah 6:9-10 (which is reflected in verse 12 here), where the prophet looks back on his unsuccessful career and sees his failure as God's will.

Others admit that Mark wrote what stands, but they find the idea intolerable and wrong. Jesus, they say, clearly uses the parables to convey and elucidate truth, not to conceal it. He is not interested in transmitting secret information to a select few: he seeks to bring all people to a knowledge of the Gospel. So though we can understand why Mark could come to this curious view (perhaps at the close of a career as an apostle that did not have the success he had expected), we must reject it as a true reflection of Jesus' mind, and as out of keeping with the other things we know about his teaching.

The reader today must come to his own decision on this matter, and it will have to be based very largely on his over-all picture of Christ in the gospels.

A word should be added here about the idea of the "secret" that appears in verse 11. It is a favorite idea of Mark's, and it is responsible for both the dramatic intensity and the theological depth of his gospel. He means by this idea that the true character of Christ as Son of God and bearer of the kingdom, as suffering and dying Messiah, is not obvious to everyone. Indeed, it is scarcely obvious even to the disciples. Peter partly sees it and largely misses it in 8:29-33. And supremely, the Jewish leaders are blind to the true meaning of Christ. This is not because of mere ignorance; Mark sees it as God's deliberate withholding of true understanding. The secret must not be revealed until the proper time, until men are prepared to receive it.

Here is the best explanation for the otherwise rather puzzling advice that Jesus constantly gives to those he has cured, not to speak publicly of what has been done to them. Sometimes, it may be, this advice can be interpreted as a word of caution to avoid bringing the inevitable crisis to pass prematurely. But the best way of viewing this advice is to see it as part of Mark's over-all theological structure. Jesus knew himself to be the Messiah, and he acts out his true nature in incident after incident. But the whole picture needed the completion of the death and the resurrection. Hence the idea of the secret, part of Jesus' own teaching, is rightly underlined by Mark as he presents his full portrait of his master.

3. an interpretation of the parable, 4:13-20

Two factors have led many observers to label this an early church homily on "how to hear God's word," rather than a direct transcription of Jesus' own words. (1) It is allegorized, which Jesus rarely does with his parables; (2) from verse 17 on, there are clear references to the situation of the church in Mark's day under the persecution of the emperor Nero. The references to persecution and tribulation, the remarks about worldly cares and security choking out the original fervor, probably reflect the difficulties facing the church at the time of the writing of the gospel rather than thirty years before. But there is no reason to believe that some interpretation of the basic parable was not given by Jesus. Mark is here shaping his material so that it would speak as directly as possible to his fellow Christians under the sentence of death.

4. other parables and sayings, 4:21-34

The section in verses 21-25 is another exhortation to respond to the preaching of the kingdom. Even if the kingdom is partly hidden now, it will shortly be revealed to all.

In the little parable of verses 26-29, the kingdom of God is again compared to a seed. Here the point is that just as the growth of a seed is not a process man controls, so the kingdom of God is not a human achievement but a gift of God. But note: when the grain is ripe, man must harvest it. The kingdom of God is now ripe; it is fully present, and man is not to sit back and wait, he is to choose it. The critical time is at hand. This parable, then, is more than a description of the kingdom of God; it is a call for immediate decision.

The parable of the mustard seed in verses 30-32 has two points: (1) just as the tiny mustard seed can grow (in the Mediterranean area) into a fairly tall tree, so the humble start of the kingdom of God does not preclude a victorious ending; (2) the kingdom is now present, and all nations and peoples ("birds of the air" was a phrase used by the rabbis to mean all people, including Gentiles) may now partake of it. Verses 33-34 serve as a conclusion to this whole section on parables and their meaning.

e. a group of miracle stories, 4:35—5:43

1. the storm on the lake, 4:35-41

The disciples and Jesus now cross the Sea of Galilee, from the west to the east shore. The detailed description here suggests an eyewitness account. A number of boats set sail; in one of them, Jesus goes to sleep on the steersman's cushion in the stern. A lake storm blows up, and the disciples rouse Jesus with a slightly bitter question. He speaks a word to the winds and the waves, and the storm subsides. He then rebukes the others for their fear, which he defines as lack of trust in God's care. They in turn respond with another kind of fear, a sort of awe in the presence of the one they only dimly understand as their Lord. The disciples' question in verse 41 presupposes, in Mark's mind, the answer: This is the Son of God at work. The contrast between faithless fear and genuine fear of the Lord is instructive. This story must certainly have served as a message of hope to the storm-tossed church under persecution in Mark's day.

But this story is also what we call a nature miracle, and it is difficult for us today, even after we have understood its original meaning and use. The healing miracles are hard enough, but there are some things in our experience that help us start on an understanding of them. The details of this story, on the other hand, seem incredible to modern man. What are we to say about it?

Some have tried to rationalize it. What Jesus really calmed, it is said, is the storm of fear in the disciples' hearts. Or, the whole thing was coincidence, even though the disciples wrongly assumed a cause and effect relation. This sort of explaining away gets rid of modern difficulties well enough, but it will hardly do, for the good reason that it departs from the simple sense of the text, which interprets the stilling of the storm as a miracle of divine providence, and as such we must deal with it.

To be sure, the ancient world was not inclined to think of the universe as bound by what we call "natural law," and so it did not have the problem with miracles that a scientific age has. What are stumbling blocks for us were merely evidences of God's action for them. But this story is really about God's power and his care for men, and not mainly about a miraculous calm. And surely we do not believe any less in the power and love of God for men than did biblical man.

Don't we pray for natural events to come to pass? For the safety of travelers, for rain, for healing of loved ones? Do we believe that God raised Jesus Christ from the dead? If we really believe that in Christ God was truly active and present, does this story present insuperable difficulties? In any case, we must be careful that we allow our Christian presuppositions to have as much weight in our reading of such narratives as we allow our modern scientific ones. Our real understanding of this story, and of others like it in Mark, will emerge not as we ask the question: "Can natural laws be broken?", but only as we reflect on a far more fundamental question: "What do we mean by Jesus Christ as Son of God?"

2. *the Gerasene madman, 5:1-20*

Here is another story of an exorcism, but one with more details than usual, and more difficulties. We are in Gentile territory; it is unlikely that a herd of pigs would be found on Jewish land. On the east shore of the lake Jesus meets a maniac who had been ostracized from his village and forced to live in the cemetery on the outskirts of town. The man sees Jesus, runs to him, and in fear and awe falls at his feet. Again the demons (that is, the demon-possessed man) recognize the divine status of Christ. The man seems to discern in Jesus' wholeness a threat to his brokenness, and implores him to leave him alone. My name is Legion, he remarks bitterly, which means that he has not one but many demons in him.

It seems that the man tries to compromise with Jesus: don't send any evil spirits out of the country, send them into the pigs. (Observe the confusion of pronouns here; "he" and "they" are mixed up together; the man is both one with his demons and apart from them.) Jesus does so, and the pigs tumble down a cliff into the sea.

The report of this spreads at once, and the townspeople come to observe the cured man. They are now, it seems, afraid of Jesus rather than the ex-maniac; if such a man could destroy swine, what else might he do? He is asked to leave. The man himself asks to come with Jesus, but instead he is told to return home (to a Gentile town, remember, which explains why there would be no danger in proclaiming the cure) and tell people what *God* has done for him. Instead, he tells people what *Jesus* did. (The Decapolis, in verse

20, was a league of ten Greek cities stretching from Damascus to the Arabian desert.)

One problem in this is the sending of the demons into the pigs. Did Jesus deliberately will this? A humanitarian might object that such an act was unnecessarily cruel to pigs. But to the Jew and to the early Christians who had been Jews the pig was unclean. And if the demons had not been sent into the pigs, it was believed, they would have entered into some other person.

Although the vivid details of this story give it a ring of plausibility, there may be elements of folk legend in it that attached to it before it came into Mark's hands. But behind the difficult details of this story, a basic truth stands. Jesus Christ, then and now, bears a unique divine power that is able to heal all kinds of human brokenness and distortion. We, like the demoniac, may be afraid to be made whole; but when this fear is overcome, wholeness, health, salvation are readily available.

3. the daughter of Jairus, and the woman with the flow of blood, 5:21-43

a. Jairus' daughter: introduction, 5:21-24

Jesus crosses back to the western shore, and a distinguished leader of the synagogue approaches him for help. The man's trust appealed to Jesus, and he goes off with him.

b. the woman with the flow of blood, 5:24-34

On the road to Jairus' house, a great crowd collects and follows Jesus. Among them is a woman with a chronic hemorrhage who had heard of Jesus and who decided to push her way through the crowd to touch him. (Notice how Luke the doctor, in 8:43, tones down Mark's disparaging reference to the medical profession when he writes up the same story.) She approaches him fearfully because she was unclean according to law, and her touch had made Jesus unclean as well. Note that it is the woman's faith—her boldness and trust—that Jesus describes as the means of the cure.

We cannot wholly explain this story; the vivid details give it an authentic flavor. Autosuggestion is hardly an explanation that will satisfy. Mark's explanation may well be the most plausible one: she was healed because of her confidence in the power of the Son of God.

c. Jairus' daughter: conclusion, 5:35-43

The simple conclusion to the story of Jairus' daughter serves as Mark's climax to the whole group of miracle stories that began with the stilling of the storm.

The report comes, while they are on the way to the house, that the girl has died. Verse 35 suggests that Jesus was not expected to be able to raise the dead. Silencing the professional mourners outside the house, Jesus takes the inner group of favorite disciples with him to the girl's side. She rises from the bed at his word, and he reminds them to feed her.

The question raised by verse 39 is this: Was the girl truly dead, or merely in a coma? Did Jesus believe she was really dead? Did Mark? Jesus had not seen the child, so it is hard to believe he was making a diagnosis in verse 39. Mark apparently believes, in placing this incident as a climax to the whole group of miracle stories, that this was an instance of a raising from the dead. The greatest reserve must be exercised before we explain away or rationalize what is difficult for us. The most important question, again, that this story poses is this: What is the meaning of Jesus Christ that shines through this incident?

f. a cool reception at home, 6:1-6

Jesus now leaves Capernaum to begin preaching in the villages and towns of Galilee. "His own country" in verse 1 probably means his birthplace, suggesting that Mark did not know of the tradition locating Jesus' birth in Bethlehem. The presence of the disciples suggests that the visit was not for personal reasons.

Many observers believe that verse 3 as it reads has been altered to fit in with the virgin birth tradition, and there is some evidence that the earlier version may have read: "Is not this the son of the carpenter (Joseph) and Mary?"

Because of the cool reception, it is said that Jesus could perform no healings in Nazareth. Not a physical inability, but a spiritual refusal, since the requisite faith and trust was not present. The clause beginning "except . . ." in verse 5 looks like a later editorial addition inserted to soften the suggestion of weakness on Jesus' part.

g. the sending out of the twelve, 6:6-13

This is the mission for which the disciples have been called and trained. They are sent out in pairs to heal and to preach the Gospel (verse 12). They are to travel light and to observe certain rules of hospitality. If they are not accepted, they are to leave at once. The shaking off of the dust is a symbolic gesture indicating a rejection of those who reject the message.

III. The Ministry Outside Galilee

6:14—8:26

1. Herod's fears, and the murder of John the Baptist, 6:14-29

Mark uses this section as an interlude to fill up the time during which the disciples are out on their mission. Of course, the death of John the Baptist probably was deeply significant to Jesus, and may have underscored his own forebodings about the future.

Herod hears of the mission of Jesus, and asks about him. (He is not technically a king, but tetrarch of Galilee and Perea, ruler of one-quarter of the realm of his father, the late King Herod the Great.) With a murderer's superstition, he fears Jesus as John the Baptist come to life again. After an introduction, Mark recounts what is doubtless a popular legend about John's death. The historian Josephus, writing some sixty years after the event, gives a number of different details. Here John has been imprisoned because of his opposition to Herod's adulterous marriage to his brother's wife Herodias. (We do not know if the brother was alive or dead; or, if alive, divorced from Herodias or not.) Herodias wanted to kill John, but the prophet apparently exercised a sort of fascination for Herod, and he merely imprisoned him. But Herodias seizes a chance at a party to trick Herod (probably in his cups) into decreeing John's death. Salome is the name given to the daughter by Josephus, but there is no name here. The note of remorse in verse 26 is interesting, but he keeps his promise and orders the execution.

2. the feeding of the 5,000 and its sequels, 6:30—7:37

a. the feeding of the 5,000, 6:30-44

The twelve now return from their mission, and Jesus takes them away to a quiet place for a rest. But the crowds follow along, and Jesus speaks with them until it is time for the evening meal. The disciples ironically ask Jesus if they should go into the village and buy forty dollars' worth of bread for the crowd. He takes the food he and the disciples have brought along for their meal, blesses it, and distributes it to the crowd. They are all filled, and there are twelve (symbolic number?) baskets of food left over.

The story, as Mark received it, was clearly a miracle, in spite of the absence of any note of astonishment or wonder in the narrative. But it is more than a creative miracle of God as it stands. It is also a sign, a pointer to a deeper truth (see Mark 6:52). When John writes up this incident in the fourth gospel (Chapter 6) he follows it with a discourse about the bread of life. The kingdom of God is, in other places, likened to a feast: Luke 14:16-24 and Matthew 22:1-14. And there are hints here that remind us of the last supper, so that this can be read as a kind of preview of that (compare 6:41 and 14:22).

So we cannot know whether the original event was miraculous or not. There is a note of mystery here, and it is best not to be sure of any conclusion. However, almost anything is better than the explanation one sometimes hears: that this is a lesson in sharing—Jesus began to share his food, and everyone else decided to do the same!

b. crossing the lake, 6:45-52

Jesus asks the disciples to leave the site of the feeding and after he has dispersed the crowd he retires into the hills for prayer. A storm blows up, and the disciples in the boats see Jesus apparently walking on the water. He quiets their fear and enters a boat, but the disciples still do not understand.

We have some grounds for attempting to rationalize this story, for there is no particular meaning to the story if read as a miracle. The disciples were in trouble, and what frightened them even more than the storm was the ghostly figure of Jesus himself. The picture of Jesus in the story is somewhat unreal. It may be that the disciples were some time in getting under way against the wind, that Jesus unexpectedly waded out into the shallow surf to meet them, and that he took them by surprise. The word of comfort in verse 50 is the significant part, and Mark adds his favorite idea about the disciples' slowness and immaturity.

c. landing on the other side, 6:53-56

Notice the growing popularity described here.

d. more controversy with the Pharisees, 7:1-23

This whole section concerns the nature of religious defilement, and verse 15 is the key to the whole. The passage can be conveniently broken up into three sections.

1. on the washing of hands, 7:1-8

The Pharisees, along with some visiting observers from Jerusalem, question Jesus' rejection of the fairly recent Jewish practice of ceremonial washing before meals. As is so often the case, Jesus does not directly respond to the question, but goes straight to the real issue at stake, which he rightly sees to be the authority of scribal tradition. (Mark remembers he is writing for Gentiles unfamiliar with Jewish practice, so he adds verses 3 and 4.) The quotation from scripture in verses 6 and 7 gives Jesus' position.

2. "Corban," 7:9-13

Again he gives an example of how human traditions can take false precedence over the commandment of God. The fifth commandment of Moses is this: Honor your father and mother. But you scribes, he says, fully approve when an unscrupulous son makes a vow to dedicate all his income to the temple, depriving his poor parents of their only means of support. "Corban" means "dedicated to God." So, a perfectly valid human vow of dedication can be used in an irresponsible way which breaks a far more basic commandment of God.

3. more sayings on defilement, 7:14-23

Verse 15 is the summary here, and it is a very significant passage for personal ethics. This is a decisive blow against all legalism: things or places cannot be unclean, only persons. Persons are not defiled by other things, but by themselves and their own disobedience to God. There is no inherent evil in nature, the world, or material things in the Christian ethic. Sin lies in man, and in his misuse of himself and the good things of God's creation. Compare this passage with Jesus' more detailed analysis of man's relation to material possessions in Matthew 6:19-34. Verses 18-19 are a rather unimaginative interpretation of the first half of verse 15, perhaps reflecting the ethical teaching of the early church. Verses 20-23 are a somewhat better interpretation of the second half of verse 15.

e. two healings, 7:24-37

1. meeting a Greek woman, 7:24-30

Again Jesus' search for privacy is interrupted. The harshness of the reply in verse 27 to the woman's request for help is the main difficulty here. Some find here a reflection of the early Christian (that is, Jewish-Christian) prejudice against Gentiles. Some find a genuine tension in Jesus' own mind between the claims of the Jews and Gentiles. Some find in Jesus' words merely a half-playful testing of the woman's faith. Jesus is impressed, in any case, by her clever and bold reply, and the cure is effected. This is a fairly rare instance of a cure done at a distance. But the real issue here is not healing so much as it is the relation of the Jew and the Gentile in the kingdom of God.

2. the deaf man with a speech defect, 7:31-37

The unusual gestures and the use of spittle (a traditional habit of ancient exorcists) can perhaps be explained by the man's deafness: he is unable to hear the usual word of command and healing.

The sighing in verse 34 is a trace of Jesus' profound compassion for the sufferer, and perhaps also of anger at the infirmity itself. Mark doubtless has in mind the passage describing the messianic age in Isaiah 35:5-10. So the evangelist here invites us to look beyond the relief of human suffering to a mighty act of God's chosen servant, bringing the kingdom into history and dethroning the rule of evil in the world.

3. the feeding of the 4,000 and its sequels, 8:1-26

a. the feeding of the 4,000, 8:1-10

Many scholars believe that this feeding is not a second incident of a miraculous feeding, but a variant account of the same event. Perhaps Mark intended the first feeding to symbolize the salvation of the Jews, and this one that of the Gentiles, since it takes place on Gentile soil. It is difficult to explain the disciples' question in 8:4 if there had been a recent incident similar to this.

The parallelism between the contexts of both feeding stories is interesting to note:

6:34-44,	feeding the 5,000	8:1-9,	feeding of 4,000
6:53-56,	crossing the Gennesaret	8:10,	crossing the sea to Dalmanutha
7:1-23,	controversy with Pharisees and scribes on defilement	8:11-13,	controversy with Pharisees about signs
7:24-30,	the Greek woman (throwing bread to the dogs)	8:14-21,	sayings about bread
7:31-37,	healing a deaf stammerer	8:22-26,	healing a blind man

There are also a number of differences between the accounts. Here we have seven loaves instead of five, 4,000 instead of 5,000, compassion because of the people's hunger here, compassion because they are like sheep without a shepherd in the earlier narrative.

b. the Pharisees ask about a sign, 8:11-13

Paul said (I Corinthians 1:22) that the Greeks seek after wisdom and the Jews look for signs. Here the Pharisees want some visible proofs of Jesus' claims; a tangible, and possibly supernatural, portent. Jesus refuses to give this sort of proof, though Mark clearly believes that as the supernatural Son of God he could have done so had he wished.

c. the mystery of the loaves, 8:14-21

In reading this section, regard verse 15 as a footnote: a warning to beware of the evil influence of the Pharisees and of Herod. It is probably an independent saying that was dropped in here because of the relationship of the ideas of leaven and bread.

The disciples have forgotten to bring along food for their boat trip across the sea. Jesus uses this incident to censure them for their forgetfulness about the meaning of the bread in the miraculous feeding. Here we have an interpretation that approaches the kind of thing the author of the fourth gospel does regularly. Mark shows us here how these feeding stories were understood by the early Christians. The feeding was a sign that the kingdom of God was in their midst and that God was sufficient for their needs. This story reminded the early church readers that not even the disciples understood what was happening in their midst. Perhaps, Mark is saying, some of us today do not yet understand the mystery of the loaves.

d. a blind man is healed, 8:22-26

Here is a cure much like that of the deaf stammerer; it is done in private, and spittle is used. It seemed to be a difficult cure to effect, for it required a second laying on of hands.

There is real artistry in Mark's placing this story here, following the one before. He has just told us of the disciples' blindness to the meaning of the loaves. Now he tells us here that even the blind can be made to see. The blind man saw; the disciples would come to see clearly; and Mark's readers will come to see as well.

IV. What Peter Finally Learned; the Journey to Jerusalem

8:27—10:52

1. messiahship and suffering, 8:27—9:29

a. Peter's confession; the Messiah must suffer, 8:27-33

Here is a crucial turning-point in the gospel. Jesus had not yet openly declared himself to be the Messiah, he had rather tried to "act it out" to his disciples. Now he seems to think they are prepared to go more deeply. Peter, who up to now had shown no special insight (and who likewise did not show much insight later), blurts out what many of them must have been thinking. As when the demons had recognized him, Jesus bids them all be silent about this new insight.

As soon as they have come to recognize his messiahship, Jesus takes them a step further with verse 31. For traditional Judaism "Messiah" meant the future king of Israel, powerful and victorious over all foes. Here Jesus declares that his kind of Messiah means suffering and death. The "must" in verse 31 is a divine necessity, and it comes not only from Jesus' acute estimate of the forces already set against him but also from his meditation on the great suffering servant passage of Isaiah 53 which he was beginning to see as a clue to his own ministry and life.

The idea of a Messiah who must suffer gets Peter out of his depth. He protests, and Jesus rebukes him.

Verse 31 represents the first of three predictions of the death and resurrection (the others are in 9:31 and 10:33-34). Mark places these sayings in their contexts to show that Jesus foresaw his sufferings and death, and this is certainly true. But to many it seems difficult to believe that Jesus predicted his own resurrection. The disciples do not seem to grasp these words; and at the crucifixion they flee in despair as if they had never heard them.

So here, something of the mystery of the Gospel is being dispelled. Jesus is the Christ, but in a different sense than anyone expected. A public announcement of the messiahship, therefore, without this deeper interpretation of it, would be foolhardy. The point of this section, then, is not merely that Peter confesses Jesus as the Christ; but also that to be the Christ, the Messiah, means to suffer and die.

b. the meaning of discipleship, 8:34—9:1

Here is a collection of sayings on the meaning of following Jesus. Notice their location immediately after the revelation of the inevitable suffering of the Messiah. Remember, too, the suffering that the persecuted Christians of Mark's day were having to undergo.

There are three conditions of true discipleship: self-denial is the first one (verse 34), which does not mean giving up *things*—as we try to do during Lent—but rather the giving up of our claim to control our lives and handing them to God. It is a confession that our wills for our lives need not be done, and that God's will shall be done, even if it denies what we wish. The second condition is taking up the cross. Bearing the cross has become trivialized in our day; it can often mean simply being brave when things go wrong. But in Jesus' words here, to be a disciple is to be willing to live and show forth the kind of suffering love that shines through the cross. To take up the cross is to acknowledge that discipleship may not win the plaudits of the world and bring to man the gifts of gratitude and success that the world can offer. Following Jesus is the last condition. This is not a lifeless imitation, but a decision to identify ourselves as radically as he did with both God's will and the suffering and need of men. This is a following that may lead to death. Verse 35 is the great paradox of biblical religion. "Saves" here means "seeks anxiously to preserve." Losing life does not mean merely death, but giving one's life up completely into God's hands. Verse 38 speaks of the consequences of disloyalty to Christ. The reference is to the last judgment. Does Jesus refer to the supernatural Son of man as another than himself or as himself?

c. the transfiguration, and coming down from the mountain, 9:2-13

This difficult story is sometimes interpreted as an historical incident in which the true glory of Christ was revealed to the three disciples, sometimes as a vision, and sometimes as a legend with only symbolic meaning.

It will help if we look at this as the counterpart for the disciples of Jesus' experience at baptism. Whatever happened, whatever a camera would or would not have recorded (and both a total acceptance as historical and a confident rejection as legendary are unwise), a significant moment in the disciples' understanding of Christ is portrayed. The relation of Christ to the Old Testament law and prophets is part of this new insight. Peter at first wants them all on the same level, and Mark (verse 6) apologizes for Peter's foolishness.

In verses 9-13 the disciples ask Jesus some further questions about what has happened. (Put the second half of verse 12 after verse 10; this will clear up the order a little.) They are wondering about rising from the dead, the suffering Messiah, and the relation of the Messiah to John the Baptist. The scribes have apparently been discussing the idea of the Messiah with the disciples, and their case against Jesus' claims apparently involves the fact that since a new Elijah traditionally must come as a forerunner, and since one has not come, Jesus' claims are false. But, Jesus reminds the disciples, the new Elijah has already come in John the Baptist.

d. the epileptic boy, 9:14-29

Jesus and the three disciples who were with him return from the mount of Transfiguration, and the contrast between the divine glory of Christ and the impotence of men (the remaining disciples) could hardly be more striking. The scribes and the disciples are arguing over the latter's failure to cure an epileptic boy. In the conversation with the father, the importance of faith and trust for healing is again emphasized. The honest cry of the father, "I believe, help my unbelief," proves his trust in Jesus, who takes the child by the hand and rouses him from the coma.

Jesus' reply to the disciples' question in verse 28 is instructive. Jesus is depicted in Mark as the Son of God with immediate power over the demons, yet here he says that prayer is essential in healing. This story is an important one for our whole approach to the healing miracles. They are not only wonderful works that proceeded from Jesus as Son of God. Here we see Jesus with such confidence in God that he expects the disciples to be able to heal, and we see him disappointed when they fail.

2. a journey through Galilee, 9:30-50

Here we find a rather loosely strung-together group of narratives, all more or less related to the meaning of true discipleship.

In verses 30-32 we notice the second prediction of the death. Why is it that the disciples don't understand? Is it because they are uncertain just to whom Jesus is referring as "Son of man"?

The next passage, verses 33-37, concerns the nature of true greatness. The disciples are embarrassed when Jesus learns that they were arguing about who was the greatest among them. Verse 35 gives his direct reply to this rather unattractive controversy; and the relation of this saying to the idea of the suffering Messiah is obvious. Then, summoning a little child, he makes his meaning even more vivid. True greatness means care for such helpless ones as this child; it means the wonder and humility that the child displays.

(Yet verses 36-37 are not precisely a direct answer to the problem of true greatness. Compare this story with the similar one in 10:13-16. Perhaps 9:36-37 should be the conclusion to the story in Chapter 10, and 10:15 the conclusion to the story here. Mark may have exchanged the two sayings about children.)

The story of the rival healer in 9:38-41 gives a lesson in tolerance. Welcome anyone who acts in my name, Jesus says, even though he is not an official disciple. Is there a conflict between 9:40 and Luke 11:23, or can both be true?

It is difficult to see much order here unless we assume that this is a compilation of Jesus' sayings made by the early church for instructional purposes. Verses 37-41 center around the idea of Jesus' name; 42, 43, 45, 47, and 48 (verses 44 and 46 are left out in the best manuscripts) refer to offenses or causing to sin; 48-50 center around the idea of salt.

3. on the way to Jerusalem, 10:1-52

a. on adultery and divorce, 10:1-12

In the background of this lies an argument between two rival rabbinic schools on divorce. The school of Hillel said that a man could get a divorce for the most trivial of reasons—if a wife burned his food, for example. The stricter school of Shammai declared that only unchastity was a just cause. Both these interpretations spring from Deuteronomy 24:1-4. But Jesus cuts beneath all this, and declares that Moses' permission of divorce was a concession to human sin and that according to Genesis 1:27 and 2:24, God ordains that the husband and wife shall be indissolubly one. The exceptions to this view, which we find in Matthew 5:32, 19:9, and Luke 16:18, represent the practical needs of the early church modifying Jesus' clear position stated here.

The point of the verses 10-12 is that in Jewish law a woman could be accused of adultery, but a married man could not. Jesus here abolishes the legal exemption of the man. "Against her" in verse 11 means, apparently, against the first wife.

It seems clear that Jesus' own position is accurately reflected in this account, and that it is qualified in Matthew and Luke. But how do we apply this teaching to the complex problem of divorce in the modern world? This is not simple to answer. Some would say that because of this teaching, divorce is simply and unequivocally prohibited. Others would object to this legalistic use of Jesus' words, and would say something like this: What we have from Jesus is the reminder that God's will for marriage is indissoluble union. But sometimes divorce, which is against this divine will, must occur. When it must, there is a sense in which God's will is being violated, even when it seems necessary from the human point of view.

b. on children, 10:13-16

The disciples apparently try to protect Jesus from the children who are being brought to him, and he is sharply indignant. Let them come; we can learn from them how to receive the kingdom of God. It is not the much-talked-about innocence of children (which parents might well question!) that is being commended here, but their sense of dependence and their receptiveness. This is a touching story about children, but even more, it is a parable about the grace of God.

c. on discipleship and riches, 10:17-31

1. the "rich young ruler," 10:17-22

The traditional description of this man is a composite one; "rich" is from Mark 10:22, "young" from Matthew 19:20, and "ruler" from Luke 18:18.

The man kneels before the teacher, a genuine act of reverence, showing that he is in earnest and not trying to trap Jesus with his question. Jesus refuses the word "good," not to say that he is sinful, but that his goodness is not that of God and has to be learned step by step, just as our own does. God alone is truly good, truly sovereign.

After the man says that he has observed all the commandments from his youth, Jesus looks on him with affection, and makes the final demand. But it proves too hard, and the man turns away sadly. This demand must not be taken as a general requirement of discipleship, but as a specific call to a particular man whose money stood in the way of full allegiance.

2. the danger of riches, 10:23-27

Who then can be saved? The answer is simple and fundamental: as an achievement of man, salvation is impossible; as a gift of God, it is available to all. The saying of verse 25 is a humorous exaggeration that underlines the virtual impossibility of a rich man meeting the conditions for receiving God's kingdom.

3. on rewards, 10:28-31

Peter's remark refers to Jesus' final challenge to the young man. Jesus replies that though the disciples have given up their actual families, in the new corporate life of the kingdom a new family will be given, and in the final summing-up of all things, they will enjoy peace and eternal life with God.

d. the third prediction of the Passion, 10:32-34

The details of this prediction correspond closely to the actual events of the passion week, and are probably to be understood as added by Mark for dramatic effect.

The vivid picture of Jesus striding ahead of his disciples as he makes his way to his fate (verse 32) is an unforgettable scene. Already, the final tragic shape of the drama is beginning to unfold.

e. John and James ask a stupid question, 10:35-45

Just as Peter missed the point of the first prediction of suffering and death, so James and John here completely misunderstand the nature of the kingdom Jesus has been talking about. They conceive of an earthly monarchy, and want to assure themselves of important places. (This is so unflattering a portrait of these two disciples that it cannot be anything but an actual historical reminiscence. The early church would hardly have created this incident.) You will participate in the kingdom, Jesus answers, but only by drinking my cup and being baptized with my baptism. Their ready agreement shows that they miss the identification of "cup" and "baptism" with suffering and death.

Verse 45 is the profound ransom passage, one of the few places in Mark where Jesus interprets the meaning of his own death. Notice how closely the life and the death are related. During the life of Jesus, serving, and not the demand to be served, was the central fact; the death is the final description of the meaning of his life. Behind the idea of ransom is the idea of men in captivity or, as we would say today, kidnapped by sin. Men cannot free themselves, just as a kidnapped victim is not free to release himself, but must wait for the ransom to be paid. The life, and supremely the death, then, serve as God's bearing the sins of men, taking them from men, so that they are no longer bound but free. Here again Jesus sees his own death not only as part of his story, but primarily as the decisive part of a story about God and what He is doing for men.

f. blind Bartimaeus, 10:46-52

The trip to Jerusalem continues. Bartimaeus gives Jesus a messianic title, Son of David, for now the secret is beginning to leak out. Many try to quiet him, but Jesus does not. In verse 51 Jesus presents the same question to the blind man that he had put just before to James and John (verse 36). It is instructive to compare the two responses. Perhaps Mark wants the reader to see that it is the disciples who are truly blind, and that the blind man has true faith and trust.

V. In Jerusalem Before the Passion

11:1—13:37

1. before the teaching begins, 11:1-25

a. the entry on a donkey, 11:1-11

This entrance into the city is an act of conscious and profound symbolism. Some commentators have compared the entry, the cleansing of the temple, and the last supper to the symbolic gestures of the Old Testament prophets. We are reminded of Jeremiah (Chapter 19) breaking a bottle before his people to symbolize the "breaking" of Jerusalem which he had predicted. The event here has been carefully planned by Jesus, and it may be that the messianic prophecy of Zechariah 9:9 is in his mind. Mark does not refer to this prophecy, though Matthew does in 21:4-5.

It is not so certain that the crowd understands this entry as messianic. The quotation from Psalm 118:26 in verse 9 was employed as a greeting for any pilgrim coming to a religious festival; verse 10 does refer specifically to the messianic kingdom, but the people probably have in mind the popular political hope. Perhaps Jesus chose this mode of entry to reveal the nature of his messiahship to those prepared to see it, and to conceal it from the rest.

We are in the midst of a scene of considerable tension. The crowd seems aware of some sort of impending crisis; the disciples are bewildered but following along; the authorities are prepared to strike at any moment; and in the midst of it all is a solitary, determined, and no doubt sorrowful, figure determined to press through to the end.

Verse 11 makes ready for the cleansing of the temple. Jesus apparently stays at Bethany from Sunday to Wednesday of the last week.

b. the cursing of the fig tree, 11:12-14

This is a difficult story, not merely because it is a nature miracle, but because of the rather petulant picture it draws of Jesus, withering a tree because it was not bearing fruit several months before its normal time. Probably the best explanation is that originally this was in the form of a parable, describing Israel as a withered tree that no longer bears fruit (see Luke 13:6-9). But in the process of oral transmission it became transformed into a narrative of an actual historical event. Mark puts the story here, in any case, to point to the coming events as decisive proof of the barrenness of the old Israel.

c. the cleansing of the temple, 11:15-19

Jesus now enters into the forecourt of the temple (sometimes called the court of the Gentiles, for it was the only place the non-Jew was allowed to pray). He drove out the officials who sold purified birds for animal sacrifices and the money-changers who exchanged (at a good profit for the priests) the popular Roman money for the Jewish coin which alone could be used for the temple dues. The action is more than that of a religious reformer protesting against corruption. It is also an act of messianic symbolism for those able to understand. In Malachi 3:1 we read: ". . . the Lord whom you seek will suddenly come to his temple; the messenger of the covenant in whom you delight, behold, he is coming, says the Lord of hosts." So here the cleansing is a symbol of the coming of God's new covenant in the person of his chosen Messiah. Notice that Jesus does not hesitate to use force to accomplish his purpose. How does this action fit in with Jesus' words about nonresistance to evil in Matthew 5:39 and love of enemies in Matthew 5:43-44?

d. the fig tree—results; and sayings on prayer and faith, 11:20-25

Verses 20-21 present the conclusion to the fig-tree incident. To this, Mark has attached a loose collection of Jesus' sayings. The context is unfortunate. Doubtless Jesus had often spoken of faith in God, but as a response to the cursing and withering of the tree, the saying in verses 22-23 takes on a trivial flavor. Of course, Verse 23 is not meant to be taken literally. This is simply a way of saying that with faith in God men can perform what seems impossible. Verse 25 reflects a knowledge of the Sermon on the Mount (Matthew 6:14) and suggests that it was known in some form in Rome in the 70's.

2. teaching in Jerusalem, 11:27—13:37

a. a series of questions from the Pharisees and others, 11:27—12:34

The apparent purpose of this series of questions was to trap Jesus into a premature and public avowal of his messiahship, and thus into an act of blasphemy for which he could be arrested.

1. what is your authority?, 11:27-33

The priests, the teachers, and the high-ranking members of the Sanhedrin or ruling court confront Jesus. Their question is a menacing one, not for information. Jesus replies by asking another question, about John the Baptist. Was God with John or not? If they said no, the people who liked John would be offended. If they said yes, they'd have to admit that God was inspiring Jesus as well.

2. parenthetical story of the wicked tenants, 12:1-12

This can be read both as a forthright advance accusation against the Pharisees as murderers (12:7-8), and also as a prediction of the rejection by God of the Jews (verses 9-10). The story becomes vivid when we make a few identifications in the allegory: the vineyard is Israel; the owner is God; the tenants are the Jews; the servants are the prophets and perhaps John the Baptist; the son is Christ.

3. may God's people pay tribute to a worldly state?, 12:13-17

This incident refers to a poll tax which all Jews under Roman occupation had to pay. After the somewhat obvious flattery of verse 14, they put the question to him. It was probably a burning question, for some of the extreme Jewish nationalists were against the tax, though the Pharisees on the whole supported it. A "no" would have given the Jews a chance to portray Jesus to the Romans as seditious; a clear "yes" would have had a bad popular effect on the ordinary man. Jesus' answer refers to this particular issue, and cannot be taken as a general guide to all the problems of political responsibility. Jesus was no revolutionary; the tax was only twenty cents a year; the coin is Caesar's anyway—why not let him have it! Other situations might arise when giving Caesar what is his might compromise allegiance to God, but this is not one of them. In such cases, "We must obey God rather than men" (Acts 5:29) would represent a part of the truth that needed stressing. A good political ethic should have both Jesus' word here, and the word from Acts.

4. do the dead rise?, 12:12-27

The Sadducees were priestly aristocrats, quite conversative, rejecting many of the theological innovations, like belief in the resurrection of the body, which the Pharisees affirmed. To understand the challenge here, we should refer to Deuteronomy 25:5 where the law of levirate marriage is set down: if a man dies without children, his brother must marry the widow. The Sadducees take an extreme case to challenge Jesus' belief in the resurrection.

Jesus responds with a double accusation. The Sadducees are ignorant of the scriptures (a telling blow, since they based their denial of the resurrection on the silence of the Torah, the first five Old Testament books), and they do not trust the power of God. Verse 25 indicates that the future life is a different order of existence from the present. "Like angels" simply means in perfect communion with God. He quotes, to make his case, from that part of the Old Testament which the Sadducees took as authoritative, in this case Exodus 3:6. If God is rightly called the God of the living, and if he is also the God of Abraham, Isaac, and Jacob, then these patriarchs must be said to be living with God.

This is a rather polemical answer, but it is effective. Its real significance lies in the fact that Jesus bases the hope for immortality not on something inherent or immortal in man, but on the power and grace of God.

5. *what is the chief commandment?, 12:28-34*

Here the questioner seems friendly, genuinely asking for information. When we recall that the rabbis distinguished 613 different commandments in the law, we can understand why an earnest Jew might ask such a question.

Jesus responds by citing two separate Old Testament passages, Deuteronomy 6:4 and Leviticus 19:18, which had not before been put together in this way. Verses 29-30 are from the Shema, the prayer which every pious Jew repeated daily. The enumeration of the various faculties merely stresses the total claim of God on man.

"As yourself," in verse 31, has always given trouble. Is this really a third commandment to love the self? Or is Jesus taking our extreme but misdirected self-love as an example of the intensity of love which ought to be directed to the neighbor? Is he saying: Love your neighbor with all the concern and passion with which, as a sinner, you now love yourself?

b. the Messiah is not David's son, 12:35-37

When we remember that the Son of David type of messianic thinking had a strongly political and nationalistic flavor, we can see why Jesus rejects certain ways of thinking about the Davidic descent of the Messiah.

c. against the scribes, 12:37-40

Having rejected some of the scribes' teaching, having just praised a sympathetic scribe's response, Jesus here turns to a criticism of their religious practice, making a devastating attack on religious professionalism. "Devouring widows' houses" probably refers to some form of financial gain based on spiritual influence over pious women, perhaps involving persuasion of the ladies to turn over their property to the clergy.

d. the widow's offering, 12:41-44

Jesus knows how much money is put in the box not because he had supernatural knowledge but probably because the amount of the gift was called out by the priests.

e. the apocalyptic discourse, 13:1-37

Most observers agree today that this chapter is a composite one, containing some general apocalyptic material from Mark's own time, as well as some genuine reflections of Jesus' own teaching. But just what does apocalyptic mean? It is a particular way of thinking about the present and the future, and it can be contrasted with the prophetic type of thought. The prophet knew that God was acting here and now, in the present events of history, and he occasionally spoke of God's action in the immediate future. Apocalyptic, we might say, is prophecy become radically pessimistic. When the present state of history and culture looks unusually black, God's immediate action in it is not so clearly seen, and the apocalyptic thinker looks far into the future, finding his hope and resting place there. His pessimism is so acute that he feels God can act only by means of some cosmic catastrophe and, instead of describing God's action now, he describes the details of that future catastrophe. Even if God does not seem to be in control now, the apocalyptist in effect says, in the final days He will be Lord of all things. We might say that the current fascination that science fiction has for some people lies just at this point: frustrated with politics and with the problem of the immediate future, man may turn to the catastrophe of the end, and speculate about what will happen then. If politics is secular prophecy, science fiction may well be called secular apocalyptic.

Let us turn to this elusive Chapter 13. The early church historian Eusebius mentions in his writings an "oracle" that warned Christians in Jerusalem to flee at the start of the Roman siege of that city in A.D. 70, and verses 6-8, 14-20, 24-27, could very well be part of that oracle rather than words of Jesus.

The whole chapter falls into the following divisions:

(1) Jesus' prediction of the destruction of the temple, verses 1-2

This was Herod's temple, begun in 20 B.C., and said to be a beautiful building. It was destroyed in A.D. 70.

(2) introduction to the discourse, verses 3-4

The disciples question Jesus about his prediction, and his response is the discourse proper. But instead of speaking of the fall of the temple, Jesus gives a detailed account of the events leading up to the end of the world.

(3) the first stage of the drama, verses 5-13

First, false messiahs will appear, claiming man's allegiance. Then will follow war, earthquakes, famines. This order of events is quite common in both Jewish and Christian apocalyptic writing of this kind. The sayings here have always been fertile ground for Christian groups predicting the end of the world after every historical catastrophe.

(4) the second stage, verses 14-23

An act of outrage to the temple is described. The "desolating sacrilege," of verse 14, refers to Daniel 9:27 and 11:31 where the pagan pollution of the temple by Antiochus Epiphanes is described. It is not clear here just what sort of act is being predicted, perhaps some sort of violence done by one of the expected false messiahs.

Observe that verses 15-18 can very easily be understood as words of warning to Christians in Jerusalem under Roman attack, rather than as warnings about the end of the world. There is some reflection of Daniel 12 here.

(5) the final stage, verses 24-27

Here the climax, a cosmic catastrophe followed by the coming of the Son of man, is described. This section is composed almost entirely of Old Testament quotation and paraphrase, and is too unoriginal to be taken as exact words of Jesus.

(6) conclusion to the chapter: on watchfulness, verses 28-37

Placed here at the end of this chapter, these warnings are made to speak of watchfulness in the face of the coming Son of man. Verse 28, however, could originally have been a saying of Jesus preparing the disciples for the crisis of his own ministry. Verse 32, suggesting that not even Jesus himself knows the time of the final consummation, must be genuine, as the early church would hardly have invented this admission of ignorance. The little parable in verses 34-36 may originally have been a word of Jesus preparing his disciples for the interval between his death and resurrection.

Thus, this chapter seems to contain some general apocalyptic material that was possibly used by the church in preparation for the destruction of Jerusalem, as well as some authentic sayings of Jesus, uttered in one context, but placed by Mark in the setting of the final consummation. The chapter as a whole presents many difficulties, but, in an age when persecution and catastrophe are not unknown to the church, it is not irrelevant; and the whole of it speaks movingly of the power of God and of his concern for his people even in the worst of times.

VI. The Passion and Resurrection Narratives

14:1—16:8 (9-20)

This final section is the most coherent and flowing in the whole of Mark's gospel, and this material was probably the first to be committed to writing. Only by such a detailed narrative could the pressing questions be answered: How did Jesus die, and why?

1. events leading up to the arrest, 14:1-52

a. the plot, 14:1-2

It is now Wednesday of holy week, and the priests and scribes decide to take Jesus at once, and privately, in view of the crowds gathering for the passover celebration. Jesus had many sympathizers, and a public arrest might cause an uprising.

b. the anointing at Bethany, 14:3-9

This strange story has two difficulties. First, what is the meaning of "For you always have the poor with you" in verse 7? This verse, taken out of context, has been put to irresponsible use in the history of Christianity, as if it were a divine sanction on poverty and a discouragement to all attempts to fight against it. The saying here must be understood as part of Jesus' commendation of the uniqueness of the woman's act. You are always commissioned to serve the poor, Jesus is saying. But this woman's act expresses a unique insight into my ministry and God's purpose, and therefore it is a worthy and beautiful thing. Second, what was there in the act that merited such praise from Jesus? Two things, the jar was broken, and Jesus was anointed. The word "Messiah" means "anointed one," and so the woman is confessing Jesus as the Messiah or Christ. But the breaking of the jar suggests that she knows the deeper meaning of his messiahship, that suffering and death await him. The disciples had not yet come up to this level.

c. Judas' betrayal, 14:10-11

What did Judas betray and why? These two questions have been the subject of endless debate. Perhaps he told the priests of Jesus' messianic claims; more likely (as is hinted here) he told them where and how they could find Jesus so that he could be arrested without a public commotion. (See John 11:57.)

But why? Whether he did it for the money, or to force Jesus into a situation where he could display his divine power and so bring in the kingdom by force, or out of personal disappointment at the apparent failure of the mission, or because he was evil from the beginning (but then why did Jesus call him in the first place?)—we simply do not know. (See John 13:2.)

d. preparing for the Passover, 14:12-16

It is now the next day, Thursday, and the disciples ask about preparations for the Passover meal that evening. Jesus' answer indicates that he has already made arrangements with some friend in the city, and he directs two of the disciples to the place.

e. the betrayal predicted, 14:17-21

Jesus has discerned the character of Judas, and announces the betrayal without pointing him out. Verse 21 indicates the divine necessity of the death, but also serves as a solemn warning to Judas.

f. the last supper, 14:22-25

In I Corinthians 11:23-26, we have an independent account of this incident which is remarkably similar. Only Paul mentions the commandment to repeat the rite, though (since Paul's letter is some years earlier than Mark's gospel) by Mark's time it has doubtless become so customary that it didn't need to be mentioned. The words over the bread and the wine differ slightly.

In reading this, recall three facts. (1) Jesus had compared the kingdom of God to a banquet (Luke 14:15-24), and this meal can be seen as a foretaste or a rehearsal of the full messianic banquet in heaven at the end of time (verse 25 here hints at this, too). (2) The Passover, which Mark relates to this supper (the trial and death take place on Passover in Mark, though not in John), commemorated the election by God of Israel as his special people, but Jesus had already made clear that the Jews were forfeiting this status in rejecting the Messiah. A new people is being formed; a new covenant, a new election, is being offered by God. (3) Jesus had already spoken of giving his life for "many" (Mark 10:45), and had described his suffering as a "cup" (Mark 10:38, and see also 14:36).

So this rite portrays the new life of the kingdom of God, pointing forward to the death and resurrection. He is doing here symbolically what he was to do the next day in fact. Standing before them, breaking the bread, he says, "This means my body." Pouring and distributing the wine, he says, "This means my life (the blood is the source of life in Hebrew thought), given to you."

The actions of breaking and pouring, therefore, are just as important as the words Jesus speaks. And when Christians, in many different ways, gather together to celebrate the sacrament of the Lord's Supper, Holy Communion, Eucharist, or Mass, the words and gestures together form the total meaning. We, like the disciples in the upper room, need something more than mere words about God and Christ. We need gestures to see; tangible things, like bread and wine, to touch and taste. This is one of the meanings of the Christian sacraments.

g. prediction of Peter's denial, 14:26-31

After the traditional passover hymn (part of Psalms 115-118), the little group leaves the upper room and goes out to the evening camp. Jesus has been reflecting on the effect his death will have on the disciples, and he tells them they will all flee away. He is shortly proved correct. Verse 28 indicates that only after the resurrection will they be reassembled. Impetuous Peter protests his loyalty, and his denial is predicted. (As an example of the kind of interesting detail you can discover if you turn to the commentaries, note that the "cock crow" is the name of the Roman trumpet call announcing the beginning of the fourth watch at 3:00 A.M.)

h. Gethsemane, 14:32-42

This scene needs little comment. Even at this late hour, Jesus asks that his time of suffering ("the hour") might pass by, that he not have to drink the cup of suffering, death, and even judgment (15:34 suggests something of what this "cup" really involves). After this bold request (there is no premature acquiescence in Jesus' prayer), he submits his will to God's. And the disciples sleep through it all.

i. arrest, 14:43-52

The priests, along with a hired gang led by Judas, appear. Judas identifies his master with the traditional kiss of the pupil for his teacher.

The little picture in verses 51-52 is odd. Some have thought that Mark is describing himself here; some consider that it is a detail suggested by Amos 2:16; others simply say it is a genuine, if irrelevant historical detail—genuine, for there seems to be no reason why the early church would have made it up.

2. the trial, crucifixion, and burial, 14:53—15:47

a. the trial before the high priests, 16:53-65

The trial of Jesus is in two parts: the ecclesiastical trial before Caiaphas and the civil trial before Pilate.

It is midnight now, and a group is hastily assembled to hear the evidence. Witnesses can't seem to agree—not even on the supposed prediction of the destruction of the temple. Jesus answers the high priest, declaring himself to be the Messiah and Son of God. The quotation from Daniel 7:13 in verse 62 is not a statement about the second coming, but about Jesus' ascension to God with power.

Verse 63 presents the priest responding in the prescribed way to an act of blasphemy. The charge is blasphemy, but the Jewish courts probably do not have the power of capital punishment (see John 18:31).

b. Peter's denial, 14:66-72

The vivid details here suggest that this story is a reminiscence of Peter. He moves from the courtyard to the front porch of the high priest's palace to avoid the girl's questions, but she talks to some of the bystanders who apparently recognize Peter's Galilean accent.

c. the ecclesiastical trial is ratified, 15:1

Meetings of the Sanhedrin after sunset being unofficial (14:53-65), they assemble again in the morning (Friday) to confirm the charge of blasphemy. Since they apparently cannot put him to death, they take Jesus off to Pilate, hoping to establish a charge of treason from his claim to be king of the Jews, and so to convince the governor that he is dangerous to law and order.

d. the civil trial before Pilate, 15:2-15

Pilate's first question indicates that the priests have been stressing the political aspects of Jesus' guilt. The answer in verse 2 is probably a "yes," but with the implication: "That is not my way of putting it, for I have no political or nationalistic pretensions." In any case, Pilate remains unconvinced by Jewish charges (verses 5, 10). Perhaps he was inclined at first to release Jesus, and certainly he considered him harmless. But the priests have brought a mob of supporters into the courtyard, and they are pressing for the release of Barabbas and the conviction of Jesus. Pilate is reluctant, but he is unwilling to risk a disturbance and is anxious for his popular reputation, so he finally gives in.

The relative guilt of Roman and Jew in all this has been much discussed. Certainly Mark lays the blame pretty heavily on the Jews, and is almost sympathetic to the weak and vacillating Pilate. And the other gospels give even more sympathetic accounts of the Roman judge. Perhaps Mark is interested in suggesting to whatever Roman officials who might read his gospel that the Roman power was relatively guiltless in the affair. But doubtless both groups, along with the crowd itself, are equally implicated.

e. the soldiers mock Jesus, 15:16-20

The soldiers' barracks were in Herod's palace, and here they bring Jesus.

f. crucifixion and death, 15:21-41

In Roman crucifixion, which was the penalty for slaves, the victim was compelled to carry the crossbar to the site. Then, his outstretched arms were tied or nailed to the crossbar, the crossbar attached to the upright, the feet fixed to the upright, and the cross then set in the ground and raised aloft. Death ordinarily was slow, taking as long as two or three days, and was usually caused by exposure.

Golgotha was apparently a skull-shaped hill outside the city, but its location cannot be identified today. Simon is chosen from the crowd to carry the piece when Jesus falters. The mention of Simon's sons suggests that they were known to Mark and to the church at Rome (see Romans 16:13).

Jesus refuses the drug, wishing to die with an unclouded mind (and remember 14:25). His clothing becomes the property of the executioners, and the soldiers throw dice for it (see Psalm 22:18). He is crucified—that is, nailed to the cross—at 9:00 A.M. The superscription, giving the offense, was on a chalked board over his head. The charge as written shows that Jesus was officially executed by the Romans, and on the charge of claiming to be king—

of course a distortion of the true messiahship as Mark and Jesus himself understood it.

As he hung there, some of the crowd, the chief priests, and even the robbers on either side joined in the general mockery. Of course, the Jewish taunt is true: he did save others, and he did not save himself, for his whole conception of the suffering Messiah meant that in order for others to be saved, he must not consider his own fate.

From noon until 3:00 P.M., it grew dark. This may be a symbolic touch, related to the portents often associated in the ancient world with the death of heroes (see *Julius Caesar,* Act 1, scene 3), or it may refer to an actual dust storm to which Mark gives a deeper significance. At 3:00 P.M., the terrible cry from Psalm 22:1 is uttered. Mark gives the Aramaic version, and translates it for his readers. This cry presents a problem too deep to be fully understood, but we can begin to grasp it if we find here a genuine, if temporary, feeling of desolation and separation from God. For Christians it is a pointer to the reality and the cost of Jesus' bearing the sin of the world, and even to the cost to God of his gift of salvation. The onlookers misunderstood, and think Jesus is calling for Elijah. At 3:00 P.M., after a cry of victory, he dies.

The curtain of the temple is torn (verse 38)—either a symbol of the destruction of Jewish religion and the temple itself, or of the breakdown of the barriers between the presence of God and men. The curtain mentioned served in the temple to shut off the Holy of Holies (where God was supposed to be specially present) from the sight of the congregation. Only the priest could ever enter the place. This curtain is torn at the moment of death.

The centurion heard the final cry of victory, and is impressed by the manner of Jesus' death. His remark, though not a full Christian confession, is at least a mark of admiration. Verses 40-41 serve as a transition to the burial and resurrection stories, and also they may suggest Mark's sources for the crucifixion story itself.

g. burial, 15:42-47

It was against Jewish law to leave bodies hanging overnight, and especially on a Sabbath. (It was now perhaps 4:00 P.M., just a few hours before sunset and the beginning of the Sabbath and Passover.) Joseph, a member of the Sanhedrin (probably in Arimathea, not the Jerusalem group that tried Jesus), asks Pilate for the body.

The close of the story seems to be unrelieved tragedy. No disciple is present; only a few sympathetic women look on from a distance; the last acts of piety are performed by a respectable Jew who probably never knew Jesus.

3. the resurrection, 16:1-8

Saturday at sunset, when the Sabbath is officially over, the women collect spices to anoint the body in the tomb. (Matthew and John say that the women merely go to see the body; Mark and Luke, that they go to anoint it.) Early the following morning they go to the tomb. They find the large stone rolled away and a young man (explicitly called an angel in Matthew 28:2-5, but only indirectly here) tells them that Jesus has risen from the grave. They hear that he is to appear in Galilee; and they rush out of the tomb in astonishment and fear. Mark makes no attempt to say how the stone was moved; doubtless he thought it was the work of God or of the risen Christ.

With the words in verse 8, "for they were afraid," the true text of Mark comes to an end. The Revised Standard Version includes, in the footnotes, both a longer ending (which appears in the King James version as part of the text) and a shorter ending which appears in some manuscripts. But it is agreed that neither of these endings is Mark's. Some feel that the ending (with verse 8) as it stands is what Mark intended, that it is effective and dramatic; some feel that the original ending has been lost, either because

Mark was interrupted in his composition (the persecutions?) or because the manuscript became torn off at the end.

When one compares the five different accounts we have of the resurrection (this, Matthew 28:1-10, Luke 24:1-11, John 20:1-10, and I Corinthians 15:3-7) there are a number of details that are impossible to harmonize. Mark may have allowed himself some imaginative freedom in depicting the scene—the story of the young man, for instance. What can hardly be called legendary or imaginative, however, is the double fact that the tomb was empty and that Jesus appeared to his followers after his death.

How can we interpret the fact of the empty tomb? If we say that the Jews or Romans stole the body, it would have been simple for them to put a stop to the preaching of the resurrection simply by producing it, but this they did not do. If we say that the disciples stole and hid the body, we have a picture of the whole origin of the Christian movement based on a piece of crude deception. Even Jewish commentators on this material find this hypothesis incredible.

Our remaining alternative is to say that God in fact did raise Jesus from the dead, changing his "physical body" into a "spiritual body," and in this latter form he appeared to his followers.

The transformation of the dispirited and cowardly disciples into forthright evangelists, the very existence of the church and the New Testament—these facts receive an adequate explanation only when we go beyond the general statement, "Jesus conquered death," to the explicit and factual remark that *God raised Jesus Christ from the dead.* This is scarcely an easy statement for any of us to make, for we are all modern men. And yet—though there is room for openness and even agnosticism on some of the details of the resurrection narrative—it seems certain that no qualification can be accepted of the actual, historical fact of the resurrection as a decisive and mighty act of God for man's salvation and eternal life.

PART THREE

JOHN

Introduction

1. who is John?

John 19:35 and 21:24 remind us that the disciple Jesus loved, the beloved disciple, is closely identified with the author of the gospel. This disciple is probably John, brother of James, and son of Zebedee. But is the disciple John actually the author? The evidence is not entirely satisfactory. The author was a Jew, with some familiarity with Palestinian geography and with the Jewish festivals. There are a number of touches that look as if they might have come from an eyewitness. But there are also inaccuracies of detail and description, and it is therefore better to conclude that though some eyewitness material lies behind this gospel (perhaps from John himself), the final writing and compilation were done by one who was not a participant in the events described.

Irenaeus, at the end of the second century, speaks of the disciple John as living to an old age in Ephesus and writing the gospel. But other early sources speak of another John, known as the elder, who lived at Ephesus, and suggest that he was the author. And so the evidence is inconclusive. The gospel may have been written by a disciple of the disciple John; it may have been written by the other John the elder, who was perhaps some kind of follower of the disciple John; or it may have been written by an unknown teacher of Ephesus who himself felt that he possessed a strong apostolic authority.

Scholars disagree about the relation of the author of the gospel to the author of the epistles of John, and about the relation of both to the author of the Book of Revelation. Almost certainly, Revelation is by a later hand. The Gospel according to John and the epistles are very close in style and content, and if both are not by the same author, they are both from the same general tradition of "Johannine" thought. John the elder, mentioned above, is often identified as the author of the epistles, even when he is not credited with the gospel.

Ephesus is the best guess for the location of the book, though Antioch and Alexandria have both been suggested. It can be dated between A.D. 85 and 140. We shall call the author John here, since "the author of the fourth gospel" is a cumbersome label. His anonymity is in many ways a virtue, and may be partly intentional. His purpose is not to bear witness to himself, but to something God has done. He is a great artist and a great theologian, and this is all that we actually need to know about him.

2. did these events really happen?

In John the unity of historical fact and interpretation is so inextricable that it is quite impossible to draw any sort of line between them. We probably should insist that John does not invent incidents or sayings of Jesus for the purposes of free speculation, but it ought also to be said that the concrete history of Jesus has been studied, meditated upon, and interpreted by him. Even the earlier gospel writers like Mark live in a kind of tension between what Jesus was in the days of his flesh and what he was for the church. John's basic standpoint is a little different: "What Jesus *is* to the faith of the true Christian believer, He *was* in the flesh," as Hoskyns puts it.[1] The final meaning of what he said and did may not rest on the surface of his actual history. But the meaning is there, none the less, and must be brought to the fore. John's purpose is to interpret the

[1] Sir Edwyn Hoskyns, *The Fourth Gospel* (London: Faber and Faber, Ltd., 1940), p. 35.

real meaning of Jesus' history, the meaning of the Gospel tradition as it came to him. He handles that tradition freely, but he insists that his interpretation is not imposed on the events but discovered there.

Thus the apparently simple question, Did these things really happen, is not so simple when we understand the rich meaning for the word "happen" that John insists we adopt. When we have seen that he does not invent incidents, that his main concern is with the concrete historical material about Jesus, we can pretty confidently answer "yes" to the question, keeping in mind the impossibility of separating what we call history and interpretation. The late William Temple has written to this issue in words that probably many commentators would accept:

> Each conversation or discourse contained in the Gospel actually took place. But it is so reported as to convey, not only the sounds uttered or the meaning then apprehended, but the meaning which, always there, has been disclosed by lifelong meditation.[2]

3. what is the difference between John's gospel and the synoptics?

There are considerable differences between John's gospel and the synoptics. In many ways it seems to be in a different world; and the distinctions come immediately to our attention. The ministry, in Mark, lasts just a little longer than a year; in John, three Passovers are mentioned. Mark describes the last supper as a Passover meal; John interprets the death of Christ as occurring the day before Passover, at the time the lambs were being killed in preparation for the feast. The short, pregnant words of teaching are missing in John. The miracles of the synoptics are often presented as human

[2] *Readings in St. John's Gospel* (London: Macmillan and Co., Ltd., 1945), p. xviii.

acts of compassion, done in response to faith, and to be concealed from the authorities. In John, fewer miracles are dealt with, and their episodic character is gone. Instead they are woven into the author's whole structure. They are pointers to Christ; they are signs or opportunities for faith, not results of faith.

Perhaps the most important difference between John and the other gospels lies in the way we experience the tension between the present and the future. This temporal tension points to what is technically called eschatology. Literally, eschatology is the Christian doctrine of the "last things," the final judgment, second coming, and general resurrection. In Mark, these things were still in the future; in John they are partly yet to come, partly already taking place. In Mark, the tension is between Jesus as he was for the disciples and Jesus as remembered and worshiped by the church. In John the tension between present and future is located in the very historical life of Jesus himself. ". . . the hour is coming, and now is" (4:23, 5:25) is not a contradiction, but a real insight into the mood of the gospel.

What John has done is to ignore the cruder forms of picture-thinking about the future that we found in the synoptics: the true eschatological event is the glorification of Christ in the resurrection. And for him this future event is beginning to happen now. No longer, for example, does the phrase "Son of man" have the ambiguous meaning that it has in Mark. In John it means this concrete man of flesh and blood—this man, Jesus, who is also Son of God. The primitive eschatology, then, is still present: the present time of the church is a time both of faith and hope, present enjoyment and future expectation, but in John the details are much simpler, and the uneasiness and tension are if anything more acute. Eternal life is present now (5:24); judgment is happening now (10:26-28); even though the disciples in John's gospel have trouble understanding Jesus (as they did in Mark), at the very beginning of the gospel Jesus is described by John the Baptist as "the Lamb of God, who takes away the sin of the world" (1:29).

John has no bits and pieces; nothing can easily be removed without distortion. It is stylistically a whole because it is theologically all of a piece. John is bound by a unifying purpose; he is doing one particular thing.

4. what was the purpose of John's gospel?

The reader should have in mind, as an aid to understanding the background of John's gospel, three important contemporary religious movements: Synagogue Judaism, Hellenistic Judaism, and Gnosticism.

a. Synagogue Judaism

In the synoptics, Jesus is shown in controversy with scribes, Pharisees, and Sadducees. Here, the blanket term "the Jews" is used. For thirty or forty years after Jesus' death, Christians continued to worship in the synagogue. Gradually they became less and less welcome, and had to seek out some private residence for their meetings. The controversies in John portray the arguments between the Christians and the Jews toward the end of the first century. Here the issues are Jesus' divinity and divine Sonship, his messiahship, his origin—human and divine. In the synoptics, the controversies were largely over what he said and taught concerning the law.

b. Hellenistic Judaism

In spite of the criticism of the Jewish tradition in this gospel, it remains essentially a Jewish book in flavor and background. But Judaism, well before the time of Jesus, had moved into the Graeco-Roman world, and had adopted some of the Greek (Hellenistic) categories and manners of thought. So John, a Jewish Christian, will be found in his gospel expounding the meaning of Jesus Christ partly in the language of this mixture of Jewish and Greek thought.

Direct Greek influence on the gospel has probably been overstressed in the past; the basic influence of the Old Testament has recently and rightly been stressed. But the thought-forms out of which the author moves, and to which he speaks, may be described as those of this Hellenistic-Jewish amalgam.

c. Gnosticism

"Gnosticism" is a loose and inaccurate word used to describe a heterogeneous mixture of religious beliefs that begins to come into the Graeco-Roman world about the same time as Christianity appears. Its origins are obscure, but it is in part derived from Babylon, Egypt, and Persia, and it includes magic, astrology, and speculation. Now gnosticism is a religion which takes the need for salvation seriously, and it presented a real problem to Christians, for much of its teaching seemed to parallel the Christian. Gnosticism is dualistic; that is, it distinguishes a spiritual world above from the lower and unreal world of matter and body. Man has a fragment of the divine life in him, but he is imprisoned in the evil world of matter, and redemption is a movement away from the body and this world, away from the fear and determinism that bind him. The epistle to the Colossians, Revelation, and I John, all bear signs of dealing with this position. Whatever external marks of similarity John may have with gnosticism, he attacks the basic gnostic position with great force: namely, that Jesus Christ could not be a true and complete man; that the Son of God could not have suffered and died. To say that the word became flesh (1:14), to insist on Jesus' thirst and weariness, and the reality of his death (20:27), is to argue directly against the basic gnostic idea of the unreality of this world. The emphasis in this gospel on the flesh of Jesus is partly determined by John's conscious repudiation of gnostic interpretations of Christianity.

So much for the background. Just what is the intention of John in writing his gospel? What was his purpose or theme? Many of the traditional answers fail to satisfy. If we say that this is only a mystical or spiritual meditation on the meaning of Jesus, we come up against the insistence on the very unspiritual idea of the flesh of Jesus. If we say that this is the work of an eyewitness, rearranging the historic events of Jesus' life in a new way, we come up against the idea that the flesh by itself means nothing. Call it Greek, the Hebraic character strikes us; call it a mixture of interpretation and history, and it is impossible to draw the line of distinction.[3] The gospel does not seem to come to rest in any known category. It eludes us.

Perhaps we are better off if we say that John's main purpose is to witness or point to the true meaning of Jesus Christ (20:31), both to confirm the faith of the believer, and to commend it to the outsider. The primitive Christian tradition, enshrined in the synoptic gospels, speaks about Jesus proclaiming the Gospel of the kingdom. For John, Jesus *is* the Gospel. The truth that lies concealed like a secret in Mark, is now openly stated. In Jesus, the holy God has come into the life of sinful man, into the flesh and sin of history itself. Man cannot know God, John says again and again (1:18, 3:13, 5:37), but Jesus Christ has made him known.

To John, the primitive tradition of the synoptics was too fragmentary and piecemeal. Men could wander in it and pick and choose. This tradition needed to be reshaped and presented in its decisive clarity. The key to John's achievement is the tension between ". . . unless you eat the flesh of the Son of man and drink his blood, you have no life in you" (6:53) and "It is the spirit that gives life, the flesh is of no avail" (6:63). The basic meaning of the primitive faith *is* Jesus Christ in his concrete historical life and death. But unless we see that the Spirit (God) is acting in this flesh, we shall miss the central clue. John simply points to this man of flesh, and invites us to respond to him.

Our task here will be simply to see what it is that John stresses. We shall spend little time trying to unravel the complicated ques-

[3] See Hoskyns, *op. cit.*, p. 129 f.

tion of history and interpretation, Is this Jesus or the early church speaking? Even if we could disentangle eyewitness account from interpretative addition, it would tell us little. The author's purpose, upon which he invites us to concentrate, is to declare that Jesus Christ actually was, from the beginning, what the church discovered him to be.

I. Prologue to John's Gospel

Chapter 1

1. the prologue itself, 1:1-18

Mark began with the baptism of Jesus; Matthew and Luke, with the birth. But both these beginnings could be confusing, so John begins at the true beginning, with creation itself. The reflection of Genesis 1 is deliberate. For a true understanding of Jesus we cannot begin with one moment in his life, but with God at the beginning.

In the beginning was the word, the *logos*. Just what does this word mean? Many things. It has a complex genealogy, and this richness is probably intended by the author. To the Greek, the Stoic primarily, logos meant the rational structure of the universe. In the Old Testament, *word* means the creative word of God, present both in creation and given to the prophets to speak. It is God's action, God's power, God's purpose. In the Jewish thinker Philo, about the time of Jesus, we find that the Greek and Old Testament meanings are fused into one, though there is no reason for assuming that John was influenced by this fusion.

In Proverbs 8:22-31, we find the idea of God's wisdom used in a way similar to the way in which *word* is used here. God's wisdom is a personalized entity, actually a portion of God extended into the world. In the New Testament, of course, the Gospel is occasionally referred to as the word of God (Luke 8:11, I John 1:1). The Christian reading this prologue would also remember—and perhaps this is as important as anything else—that Jesus himself spoke words, and these words are interpreted as the very words of God himself.

So, this elusive word will mean something both to the secular mind, to the Jew, and to the Christian. Perhaps this ambiguity is deliberately intended by John; he is saying to Greek, to Jew, and to Christian: Jesus Christ is the fulfillment of each of your traditions and hopes.

Today, we can get closest to an understanding of this key word in the prologue if we interpret it as the outgoing, creative action of God in visiting and redeeming his people. This purpose was part of God from the very beginning; there may be more of God than this (though this is perhaps all man can know), but the very divinity of God is defined by this purposeful activity toward men (verse 1). And verse 3 reminds us that there are no intermediaries or levels between this redemptive God and his creation, as the gnostics held. The world is good because it was made by this creative, active God. Part of the divine activity, perhaps the decisive part for John, is that of imparting life, a full life here and now, and eternal life which begins here and now. This life is the means by which men see and understand; it is, therefore, the light of men (verse 4).

There is still darkness; man is often unable to see the light; he is still in unbelief. But this light, the divine gift by which man can see Christ, is shining in the midst of this darkness. It is shining (note the present tense of "shines"; it began to shine in the beginning; it shone with special power in Christ, but it is still shining now) not as a flickering candle but as a mighty searchlight hunting out man lost in his darkness. The word for "overcome" has a double meaning: here the meaning is that the darkness has not destroyed the light, and also that the darkness (unbelief in general and the Jews in particular) has not understood it.

Verses 6-8 briefly describe the function of John the Baptist. Gone is the story of his preaching and teaching; here his function is radically narrowed so that he has become merely a pointer to the light that is in Christ. His function, like that of the author of the gospel, and like the Christian's of any time, is simply witness.

With verse 9 we return to the argument of verse 5. In Christ, the logos or word, the life, the light, came into the world, but the world did not understand him. Not even his own people, the Jews, understood him. But some did, and to those he gave a new status as sons or children of God. This new beginning (it is called a new birth in the story of Nicodemus in 3:1-12) is not made by man; it is God's gift.

The word became flesh (verse 14). This has already been assumed in verses 9-13, and now it is openly declared. The word had been with God from the beginning; it had been spoken through the prophets of old; but this is something new. It has now come into history itself, to be seen and touched by men. (Compare the opening verses of I John and the epistle to the Hebrews.) The word "dwelt" really means that the word has built its tent in our midst, has come to live or to "tabernacle" with us; the reference is to the sacred presence of God in the Old Testament, described as his tabernacling presence. (See Exodus 25:8-9, 40:34.)

"We beheld," John writes. This is a past seeing, not a present one. The presence of Christ when John writes is not the same as it was in the days of his flesh. Then it was seeing of one kind; now it is still seeing, but different. "We" beheld; the true disciples, the true followers; not everyone. For the high priest didn't see; Pilate didn't; Judas didn't. What was seen? His glory. What does this mean? The same as "light" earlier in the prologue. We saw in him the light that made us able to know God. We saw in him the very power of God himself.

In verse 18, John introduces one of his favorite themes: man cannot see God, know God, have a direct union with God. But he is not thereby lost; we can know Christ, and Christ makes God known. "In the bosom of the Father" is an image of neither romantic nor parental love. It refers to the companionship of a common meal (see comment on 13:23-25, page 178).

The prologue is at an end, and the entire gospel—indeed, the entire Christian story—is here summed up. In Jesus Christ man has access to the living God himself, and through this access come light and life, grace and truth. The rest of the gospel simply expands this affirmation.

2. the witness of John the Baptist and his disciples, 1:19-51

The Jewish authorities send a delegation to discover the status of John the Baptist. He responds with a threefold denial: he is neither the Messiah, Elijah (Malachi 4:5), nor the prophet (Deuteronomy 18:15). He has no positive messianic significance. He does describe his status in relation to a part of the Old Testament, but even this has the effect of reducing his meaning to a mere voice pointing beyond himself. It appears from verses 19-28 that John does not yet know that Jesus is the Messiah. He is asked about his rite of baptism; he defines it only in terms of purification and preparation for what is to come. But who is to come he does not yet seem to know.

With verses 29-34 the object of John's witness is revealed to him. He does not find it out himself, it is given to him. In Mark, only Jesus is aware of the meaning of his own baptism; in verses 32-34 God reveals the meaning to John. Now John the Baptist points explicitly to Jesus, and describes him in three ways. He is the Lamb of God (29), the one who baptizes by the Spirit (33), and the Son of God (34).

To describe Jesus as the Lamb of God is to go beyond the traditional messianic names and to make a statement about the meaning of his voluntary death. In the Old Testament, the lamb is both the victim provided by God as a substitute for Isaac (Genesis 22:8) and a means by which sin is removed.

Verses 35-51 describe the call of the first disciples, though Jesus directly calls only Philip (43). This should be read in connection with the call of Peter and Andrew, James and John, in Mark 1:16-20.

The next day John the Baptist again bears witness to Jesus as the Lamb of God, and two of John's disciples leave him and follow Jesus. One of these first two is Andrew, but who is the unnamed second? Is it in fact John, the beloved disciple, on whose witness this gospel is traditionally said to be founded? Andrew, having obeyed Jesus' call, gets his brother Simon Peter, and brings him to Jesus. This is almost all we ever hear of Andrew in the New Testament; he performs the humble act of bringing another man to Jesus. This is why he has been taken as the patron of the missionary activity of the church.

Jesus calls Philip directly, and Philip bears witness to Nathanael. Nathanael does not come from John the Baptist's followers but from Israel—indeed, from the tradition of Jewish skepticism. How can the Messiah come from tiny and insignificant Nazareth, he asks. His questioning mind, his study of the Jewish law (the perplexing reference to the fig tree in verse 48 probably points to the fact that Nathanael was a student of the law, for the rabbis used to say that the best place to study the law was sitting under a fig tree) prompted Jesus to praise him as a true Jew and an honest man (1:47). It is not clear whether Jesus is meant to have some special foresight about Nathanael, or whether he was known to him already. Nathanael responds to Jesus' discernment, and calls him Son of God, but limits his rule to Israel (1:49). His insight is not yet complete, and Jesus tells him he will understand even more. The reference to the angels in verse 51 is from the vision of Jacob in Genesis 28:10-17. The verse describes what Nathanael will be able to say: that the concrete man Jesus is the one on whom God has descended and acted; that Jesus himself is the unique relation between heaven and earth. Jesus does not promise Nathanael a vision, but an insight into who he, Jesus, truly is.

This second prologue in narrative form ends, as does the first (verses 1-18), with the positive statement of Jesus Christ's unique relation to God (compare verses 18 and 51).

II. On the Meaning of Jesus Christ

2:1—12:50

1. Christ as bearer of a new order of life, 2:1—4:42

a. two signs pointing to Christ's meaning, 2:1-22

1. the wedding at Cana, 2:1-11

The form of this story is that of miracle, a creative act of God whose methods cannot be described. More important, the purpose of this story is that of a sign, a pointer to the meaning of Jesus Christ. What meaning is intended here, is the question the reader should ask.

In 1:43 Jesus had decided to go to Galilee, and he has now arrived. He attends a wedding feast with his disciples, and his mother observes that the wine is running out. Jesus' reply to her (2:4) is not petulant, but it does point to the fact that the time of her authority over him is at an end. His "hour," he says, has not yet come. The reference is to the time of death and glorification. So until that time, his acts and his words must be in the form of signs or pointers to what his meaning is and is to be. The servants draw from the water jars (used for the Jewish rites of purification) and discover that the water has become good wine. The guests do not know what has happened; the servants know, but do not understand; the disciples know, partly understand (see 2:11, 22), and believe.

It is just possible that there are pagan sources for this story, perhaps from the rites of Dionysus. But it is more important to recall two facts from the synoptic tradition. In Mark 2:19 the disciples with Jesus are likened to guests at a wedding feast. And in Mark 2:22 the Gospel is compared to new wine that breaks old wineskins. This latter passage really gives us the clue to this sign. The water of purification (the Jewish faith) is inadequate, just as John the Baptist's baptism by water was inadequate (1:26), and Jesus' function is to give the true interpretation to the old rites. He does this by bearing the power of God ("glory" in verse 11), to which all men, like the disciples in the story, should respond in faith.

2. *the cleansing of the temple, 2:13-22*

This event takes place in Mark (11:15-19) at the beginning of the final week. John places it at the start of the ministry. It is not necessary to conclude that John had some better chronological source than Mark; he is always more interested in the meaning of Jesus' acts than in their setting, and his reason for placing the cleansing here is surely theological. The story of Cana is a story about purification, and the relation of the old and the new. That is the theme here as well. The disciples don't see this meaning; verse 17 suggests that they merely see the actions of a prophetic reformer. Indeed, unlike the miracle at Cana, the disciples don't really understand this incident at all. The Jews respond to Jesus' words in verse 19 (similar to Mark 14:58) by assuming he intends to destroy the actual temple and rebuild it in three days. The disciples later reflect on the saying, and interpret it as a prediction of the resurrection (2:22). Jesus presumably means that his mission in fact involves a destruction of the old way of worship, and a new way of approach to God, and in that sense, a new "temple" is indeed present (see 4:21-24).

b. the theme of the new birth, 2:23—3:36

In Jerusalem, apparently there were many who believed in Jesus because of the signs. But Jesus knows that belief merely because of miraculous acts is likely to be transient when it does not penetrate to the meaning behind the act. He indeed knows the depth of sin and deceit in the heart of man, and the hollowness of easy belief.

1. the dialogue with Nicodemus, 3:1-21

Nicodemus, a distinguished Jewish teacher, seeks Jesus out under the cover of night. His words of praise to Jesus (3:2) should not be dismissed as pious flattery, though they do of course fall far short of Jesus' true meaning. Jesus' response can be divided into three rather unequal parts.

In verses 3-8, Jesus' main point is that repentance is a condition of knowledge of God. This is developed in three different images—birth, baptism, and wind. You must be born anew (or from above—the word can and probably does mean both) if you wish to see (3) or to enter (5) the kingdom of God. These two references to "kingdom of God" are unique in the gospel; the phrase appears nowhere else. John avoids the idea of kingship and kingly rule, preferring sonship and eternal life; but the use here reminds us of the rich meaning of this idea in the synoptics, particularly the idea that the kingdom is present in the words and deeds of Jesus himself.

Nicodemus, for all his claims to be a religious expert, is very literal in his understanding of Jesus' saying about being born again, and points out the physical impossibility of such a thing. Birth is an extremely powerful figure for repentance and conversion, perhaps the most accurate figure conceivable. The ideas of newness, mystery, and suffering are all involved. In John 3:5-7 the figure shifts to that of baptism. Jesus says in effect that what is required is not a new physical beginning, but a new beginning from God, a new birth of the Spirit. Baptism of water, which John the Baptist has mentioned already (1:26) means purification; baptism of the Spirit means that the new beginning is a gift of God and not a human possibility. (Nicodemus is partly right, though for the wrong reasons, in saying that this rebirth is a physical impossibility. John likes to show how the Jewish literalistic misunderstanding of his words often has unintended insight.) Finally, in verse 8, he underlines his point by comparing the man of the Spirit to the wind. Just as the wind is not controlled by man, but comes from a source other than man, so the man of the Spirit is what he is, not by a human decision but by a gift that has come to him from above, from outside. Nicodemus again raises questions, and Jesus expresses his surprise that a religious teacher should not understand that repentance is God's gift.

In John 3:11-13 we get the second main point of the discourse: that an answer to the question about Jesus will not be given by scanning the heavens, but by attending to the human words and deeds of the one standing before you, the Son of man—that is, this concrete earthly man. The man of faith does not have to go up to heaven to discover God; in the Son of man, God has come down to where man is. If Nicodemus can't even grasp that, how can he be expected to understand "heavenly things"?

The third and final point of the discourse is contained in verses 14-21. It has to do with the relation of death, love, and judgment. The reference to Jesus' death is easy to miss, and it is contained in verse 14. In Numbers 21:6-9, Moses cures the people of the bites of poisonous serpents by holding up before them a standard on which an image of a serpent is attached. And so, Jesus must be "lifted up"—in glory, but "lifted up" also on the cross—to be seen by men, before they can be "cured" of their sin, and receive eternal life. The descent of the Son of man that is described in verse 13, then, is a descent that ends in a death. It is also a descent and death that defines God's love (verse 15). But if Christ's death is God's love, God's love is also God's judgment.

With verse 16, we seem to move to John's words of comment on the discourse. Nicodemus has now left the scene altogether, and we do not know the results of his discussion with Jesus, though we may pick up some hints from the other references to him in the gospel, 7:45-52 and 19:39-42.

To relate judgment to love is to say that God does not directly condemn any man; the purpose of Christ is not condemnation but salvation or life (3:17). But there is a judgment; it is not what God does to man, but what man, in his rejection, does to himself. Here is a radically new conception of the judgment of God. Notice, in verses 18-21, that this judgment is even now coming into the world. It is not merely a future superhistorical event, as in the synoptic gospels. It begins with Christ, when men reject him. Apart from Christ the light, men's deeds are their own deeds, and are evil. In Christ the light, men's deeds become true, but they are not their own deeds; they are the deeds that God has worked in them (verse 21).

2. John the Baptist bears witness to the newness of Christ, 3:22-36

Here, the relation of Jesus Christ to Judaism is dealt with once more, before the narrative moves into Samaria and to the problem of Jesus' relationship to those outside of Israel.

In Mark 1:14, Jesus' ministry starts only after John the Baptist's arrest. Here, in John's gospel, they are both at work, but separately. A Jew reports to John that Jesus is also baptizing, and that some of John's followers are going over to Jesus. As before, John makes no claims for himself. In two vivid figures he merely points to the new reality in Jesus Christ. Verses 29-30 liken John to the best man, Jesus to the bridegroom. As the best man plays only a minor role at a wedding, and as the bride (Israel?) is not his but the groom's, his only purpose is to share in the wedding joy and withdraw, once his work is done. Verses 31-36 develop the contrast between Jesus and John more fully. John compares himself to a man of the earth, Jesus to a man from above, from God. Jesus' unique witness is that of the Son to the Father; John witnesses only to the Son.

c. Jesus and the Samaritans, 4:1-42

To avoid the Pharisees, Jesus makes a journey again to Galilee, and passes through Samaria on the way. The Samaritans are partly Gentiles racially, but consider themselves the true inheritors of the Jewish tradition. The mission of Jesus beyond Israel is perhaps the main point of the story.

In verse 9, the woman is surprised that a Jew would speak to a Samaritan. But the real tension is not between Jew and Samaritan, but between Jesus as Son of God and a sinner. The paradox here is that he who asks for water is the true giver of water, and she who has ordinary water is the one who needs true or living water. The woman is irritated at Jesus' claim to be able to give her living water. She thinks he means running water from a stream in contrast to well water, and she accuses him of claiming to be greater than Jacob who dug the well because he had no access to running water. Jesus further describes what he means by living water, and now the woman asks for it. He first had asked; now she asks. But she still does not understand, for she apparently is asking for water that will not make it necessary to make the daily trip to the well.

Since she had asked for the water, Jesus offers the true and living water of eternal life. This water is forgiveness of sin, so he begins by laying bare her inner disorder. We need not bother with the question how Jesus knew these details of her domestic history.

The discussion about the true place of worship (4:20) is directly relevant to the confession of sin, for the place of worship is the place of forgiveness. Her sin being revealed, it is appropriate that she ask about the true place of forgiveness. She refers to the controversy between the Samaritans and Jews about the true place of worship; the Samaritans claimed it to be the near-by Mount Gerizim, the Jews claimed the Jerusalem temple. Jesus undercuts this argument by saying that now neither of these two places is fully adequate. The God of the Samaritans is an unknown God, while the God of the Jews is the true God. But "the hour is coming, and now is," (verses 21, 23) when the true character of the God to be worshiped will solve this ancient controversy. Prophecy is at an end, and the new age is at hand. God is spirit, but this does not mean that he is something apart from matter. In our day there is a good deal of vagueness in the way we use "spirit" and "spiritual," and we often call God spirit when we can think of nothing else to say. Here it does not mean that God is nonmaterial, it means that he is power, grace, and action, and that because of his freedom he can be worshiped at all times and in all places.

The lesser questions have been left behind: living water, sin, the true place of worship and forgiveness. The ultimate problem for the woman is the character of God who gives the water, who forgives sin, and who is truly worshiped. She rightly sees (4:25) that this is a question about the nature of the Messiah, but wrongly says that it cannot be settled until he comes. Jesus abruptly completes the discussion by declaring himself to be the Messiah. He himself is the answer to the problem of sin, worship, and the character of God.

The disciples return from buying food (4:27), and are surprised to find Jesus talking alone with a woman. The disciples bid Jesus eat; he replies that he has food, and they wonder if someone had already brought him something. Their literal misunderstanding about "food" is the same kind as the literal misunderstanding about "water" that the woman had just been freed from. Jesus declares that his food is to accomplish God's work. This leads him on to talk about the harvest. By harvest he means the understanding of eternal life; the disciples mean a literal harvest and point out that it is still four months from harvest time. But Jesus sees the Samaritans, brought by the woman, approaching the well, and he tells the disciples that the time is ripe for harvest now. He is the one who sows; the disciples are the reapers; the time to act is now. "Reaping," in the synoptics, was in the future. Here, it is to be done at once.

The story concludes (4:39-42) with a description of the Samaritans' belief, not merely on the basis of the woman's words, but because they had come to understand for themselves. The woman partly saw, then fully saw. The disciples saw only dimly. The Samaritans know fully that he is the Savior of the world.

2. Christ as giver of life, 4:43—5:47

The passage in 4:43-54 gives the first healing miracle in the gospel, the first of two in this section. The Galileans' faith is based on their having seen "all that he had done in Jerusalem." We are reminded of the faith of the Samaritans just before, which was not based on signs or miracles; and we shall see in the faith of the official (4:46-54) a faith which is tempted to base itself on a seen miracle, but which finally does not require such evidence.

This healing is done in Cana, site of the first sign of the Gospel (2:1-11). Verse 48 suggests a rebuke to a faith that needs to be buttressed by signs, but Jesus speaks the word that is requested. The man believes, however, before he verifies the efficacy of the act of healing (4:50).

The second healing (5:1-18) of the cripple beside the pool (which was apparently believed to have healing properties, hence the collection of invalids around it) relates healing and forgiveness (5:14) in a way that reminds us of the story in Mark 2:1-12. The man at first does not know who healed him, but he later finds out, and reports the fact to the Jews. They find two grounds for opposition to Jesus: he healed on the Sabbath (5:16), and, far more serious, he claims some sort of identity with God, calling him Father, and thus is guilty of blasphemy.

The accusation of blasphemy leads to the first extended discourse delivered against the Jews by Jesus (5:19-47). He begins by denying that he claims equality with God; his true relation to the Father is one of obedience and dependence. The Son works now, and will continue to work (5:20). This points, not to some transhistorical future hope, but to the immediate future in the life of the concrete historical Jesus. The greater works referred to are the raising of Lazarus (11:1-44) and perhaps Jesus' own resurrection. But if verse 19 stresses the lowly obedience of the Son, verses 22-25 stress the authority of the Son, his judgment, and his gift of life. But, as verses 25-29 go on to reveal, the real "work" of the future is the final resurrection, the final passing from death to life. In one sense it is a future event. In another sense the future event (which the synoptics emphasized more than John does) is merely a completion of the movement from sin to forgiveness, unbelief to belief, that is going on here and now, in the person and presence of the Son of man (5:27), Jesus himself.

In verses 30-47, the authority of Jesus is further defined and distinguished from other authorities which are its basis: that of John the Baptist (verses 33-35), Jesus' own works (36), and the witness and voice of God in the Old Testament (37-40). These three witnesses are the true condemnation of the Jews; their condemnation of Jesus (verse 18) is false. Their own tradition judges them. Since they hold to the law of Moses that reveals sin, why can they not acknowledge Christ's forgiveness of that sin?

This contrast between Jesus and the Jews (and the similar contrast between church and synagogue at the time John writes) gives us the true theological meaning of the two healings at the beginning of this section, and further portrays the radically new thing that is entering the world in Christ.

3. Christ as bread of life, chapter 6

This section also begins with two miracles from the synoptic tradition, and proceeds to a discourse based on them. Previously we were dealing with the unbelief of the Jerusalem Jews; here it is the unbelief of the Galileans.

In verses 1-15, John retells the story of the feeding of the 5,000 (Mark 6:35-44). John, like Mark, interprets the story as a creative miracle of God, and offers no other explanation. Note the Passover reference in verse 4. At Passover, the people eat unleavened bread and the flesh of an unblemished lamb. Without this imagery, the movement in the discourse from the idea of bread to that of flesh is difficult. In verses 14-15 the people acclaim Jesus as a miraculous giver of food and as a king. Of course, he is, but not in the popular sense; and so he quickly withdraws.

Verses 16-21 retell the miracle of walking on the water (see Mark 6:45-52), and it is interesting to note that John offers no special interpretation of it.

The rest of the chapter, 6:22-71, is the discourse itself. Verses 22-25 are a somewhat obscure explanation of how the crowd gets across the sea. In 26-40 Jesus speaks to the crowd he had fed: in 41-59 he speaks to the Jews in the synagogue; 60-71 is addressed to the disciples.

The discourse to the crowd in verses 26-40 is similar in form to 4:7-15 on the water of life. The woman becomes the Galilean; the well of Jacob becomes the manna given by Moses; and the water of baptism becomes the bread of the Lord's Supper. Jesus accuses the crowd of seeking him for ordinary bread, and not for that of which the bread is a sign. (Jesus says that the Son of man "will give" in verse 27—this points to the death and resurrection as the final seal of the gift; but he says in verse 32 that "my Father gives you the true bread," showing that the gift can now be received.) The crowds ask in verse 28 what work they must do for his bread, knowing that they have to work for their actual bread.

The answer is faith or belief in the Son; that is their work, even though it too is a gift of God (verse 29). They cite the gift of manna from Moses as part of their objection to Jesus, but Jesus will not allow this, for God himself provided even that.

In verse 30, they ask for a clear sign so that they may believe. But there can never be as clear a sign as they wish. Jesus will not so much *do* a sign as *be* one. So verses 35-40 are the only answer to their question that they will ever receive, and the answer is simple: Jesus is the true bread of life because he comes from God and does God's will. Note in verses 39, 40, and later in 44 and 54, the reference to the future resurrection. We have often noted that John, like Mark, maintains this temporal tension.

The Jews have listened to this, and the discourse directed to them in verses 41-59 is based on two main objections that they raise. The first concerns Jesus' origin. How can he come from heaven, they ask, when we know him to be the son of Joseph? He declares again that he is the bread of life, but makes it even more explicit by pointing to his flesh and to eating his flesh as the real meaning of receiving his bread. Here the Passover setting is recalled; both the death of Christ and the Lord's Supper are suggested by verse 51. This leads the Jews to their second, and even more irritated, objection: How can a man give us his flesh to eat (52)? As with the first objection, Jesus does not so much answer it as reaffirm the basis for it. The word for "eat" in verse 53 is a crude one: it means to eat the way animals do, to munch. Eating the flesh and drinking the blood have overtones of the Lord's Supper, and many scholars have tried to point out in these words the influence of the mystery religions, which often spoke about eating the body of the dying and rising savior god. But the basic meaning here, remembering that according to Hebrew psychology flesh-and-blood means simply human nature, is that eternal life comes by attending to the concrete historical words and deeds of Jesus. He, therefore, is the true bread (here is a shift back from flesh to bread); unlike the manna given by Moses, whoever eats this new bread shall be united with Christ and shall therefore "live."

The unbelief of the Jews is contagious, and in John 6:60-71 we read that some of the "disciples" began to wonder at Jesus' words: not the twelve, but some of the larger group of followers. His was a hard saying, not because it was unintelligible, but because it was offensive and coarse. True, the flesh must be eaten (6:53), but it is just as true that the flesh is of no avail (63). By themselves, the historical events of Jesus mean nothing: many saw them and did not respond. God, the spirit, must give them life; there is no life without the fleshly events, but there is no life either without God's spiritual gift of faith, the ability to discover the true meaning of the events of fleshly history. And so the real contrast of verse 63 is not between flesh and spirit (in the modern sense of nonmateriality), or between history and some realm of eternity; but between living historical reality (flesh), illumined by God's gift of faith—and dead flesh, dead events, uninterpreted and barren.

Verses 66-71 suggest the confession of Peter (Mark 8:27-30). Here, Peter confesses that Jesus' words are not merely teaching words about God, but creative and life-giving. Man does not know God; only Christ knows the Father. But man, like Peter here, can believe, not so much in God but rather in the assurance that Christ is the Holy One of God, the true and only access to God. Only if he begins with this belief, will knowledge ever be granted.

4. Christ: revelation and rejection, 7:1—8:59

a. introduction, 7:1-13

The Jewish Feast of Tabernacles was an autumnal feast of harvest thanksgiving, celebrating the miracles wrought during the stay of Israel in the desert. Jesus' brothers approach him and, like his mother in 2:1-11, ask him to use his miraculous power openly to prove himself. They show themselves unbelievers in their misunderstanding of the nature of his power and of the distinction between his public and private ministry. The apparent contradiction between verses 8 and 10 can be explained by seeing verse 8 as a refusal to go to the feast publicly; though it is possible to read it also as a refusal to "go up" at the time of the feast, in the sense of be lifted up, glorified, going up to the Father, as in 3:13, 6:62, 20:17.

Finally Jesus does go to Jerusalem, and the crowds are beginning to argue about him (verses 10-13).

b. Jesus at the feast, 7:14—8:59

1. dialogue on Moses and Christ, 7:14-24

Verse 21 reminds us that this section is a further interpretation of the healing of the cripple in 5:1-18, and a continuation of the controversy that the miracle stirred up. Jesus defends his healing on the Sabbath by pointing out that according to the law, circumcision must be done on the eighth day, even if that day falls on a Sabbath. So the law requires that the law against work on the Sabbath be broken in regard to circumcision. If it can be broken for circumcision (which is the opposite of healing), why can it not be broken for healing?

2. dialogues on Jesus' messiahship, 7:25-52

The defense of the healing is valid only if Jesus is in fact the Messiah, so this now becomes the issue. The crowds wonder whether the Jews have changed their minds about Jesus since he is apparently being allowed to speak openly. Perhaps the authorities now believe him to be the Messiah, they speculate. But they conclude he cannot be; the origin of Jesus is well-known, and the origin of the true Messiah will be hidden and obscure. In verses 28-29 Jesus enters the argument and declares that they do not in fact know his origin at all, for his origin is God whom they do not know. This effrontery provokes an attempt to arrest him; it also provokes a sort of partial belief based on the miracles, particularly the one (5:1-18) under discussion (7:31).

The half-belief of the crowds is contrasted with the unbelief of the priests and the Pharisees who now send soldiers to arrest Jesus (7:32). But they either do not or cannot, and he speaks about his departure to a place where they cannot come. The Jews misunderstand, thinking he is referring to some sort of escape, perhaps to the Jewish community in the Gentile world (verse 35). This is literally false, but true in the sense that Jesus' message does in fact ultimately "escape" beyond Israel to the Gentile world. Notice the implications of judgment in Jesus' words to the Jews about their inability to come where he is going.

The word of judgment is followed by a promise of eternal life in verses 37-39. Anyone who believes, he says, can now receive eternal life, and will ultimately receive the gift of the Spirit. This "anyone" has already included the Samaritans (4:42), and this saying may be taken as the response to his brothers' request (7:4) to manifest himself to the whole world.

These words of promise lead to further controversy about his messiahship among the crowd (verses 40-44). He is called various things, but apparently the belief that the Messiah was to come of David's line from Bethlehem remains a serious obstacle. Is it that John does not know the tradition about Jesus' birth in Bethlehem in Matthew 1 and Luke 1? Or does he refrain from using it because he does not believe it?

The soldiers sent out to arrest him in verse 32 now return to the Jewish authorities (verses 45-52), and they apparently have become infected by his words. The Jews contemptuously reject Jesus' claims and the half-belief of the crowd in him, saying (wrongly, as it happens, for Jonah was from Galilee) that no prophet has ever come from Galilee.

Note on 7:53—8:11, the woman taken in adultery

It is certain that this section is not part of John's gospel. It is more like Luke than either of the other gospels, and was apparently a piece of floating tradition that came to rest here because of the sayings in John 7:24 and 8:15. The mount of Olives and the temple locate the incident in Jerusalem and, therefore, in the final week of Jesus' life. The scribes and the Pharisees had caught a woman in the act of adultery and had brought her to Jesus: not to seek guidance on a difficult moral issue, but to trap him. The assumption is that adultery is a violation of the law of God and that the Jew has a responsibility to be an agent of God's punishment. The issue is simply this: witnesses to adultery are required by law to stone the adulterers. What will Jesus say to this law? Verse 7 is the key. Its meaning is that only a sinless one can be a true agent of God's judgment, and so Jesus refuses to allow the Jews' claim.

After the Jews leave the scene, Jesus neither condemns nor forgives. There can be no forgiveness, for there is no repentance. He does not condone her act; he merely issues a call to righteousness; she is an object of mercy, but not yet forgiven. Both judgment and forgiveness are withheld. The tension between the prohibition of judging in Matthew 7:1 and Jesus' "judgment" of the Pharisees is thus resolved in this story. He does not judge; he issues the call of God to righteousness, and judgment is brought on the sinner if he refuses this call.

3. dialogue on Jesus' witness against the Jews, 8:12-59

The first discourse against the Jews was 5:19-47, and this is the second extended one. Verses 12-20 concern the character of Jesus' witness. Darkness, we have already noted, stands for sin and unbelief; light, therefore, suggests the opposite. Not merely insight and knowledge, but forgiveness and eternal life. Again, as before, the accusation of egotism is leveled against Jesus. Jesus admits that he does bear witness to himself, but adds that his Father also bears witness to him. Jesus' witness leads to judgment; not to a judgment that he exercises, but to a judgment that comes upon all men when they reject his witness. The Jews ask Jesus where his Father is located (8:19). This is partly an accusation against him, related to the rumor that he was an illegitimate son of Mary, but it is also a theological question about his spiritual paternity. Jesus ignores the first meaning of the question and accuses the questioners of a complete misunderstanding of the character of God. A demand to be shown the concrete visibility of God will never be met directly; Christ, the Son, is the only answer to that question.

In verses 21-30 he continues to explain his relation to the Father. As in 7:33-36, the Jews misunderstand his reference to going away. Jesus means his death and glorification; the Jews think that he means suicide. Of course this misunderstanding obliquely points to a truth, for Jesus' death was a voluntary one. Note that verse 24 suggests that there is nothing inevitable about the Jewish rejection of Jesus. Indeed, verse 28 suggests that some Jews actually believed after the crucifixion. (On "lifted up," see comment on 3:14, page 157.) And verse 30 suggests that some believed even as he spoke.

Verses 31-59 seem to be spoken to those in verse 30 who partially believed. If so, this final section of the discourse is a study of the disintegration of partial belief into hostile and complete unbelief (see 8:37 and the final verse, 59). The subject of this discourse is freedom, freedom from sin (8:34) and death (8:51). The Jews don't like the suggestion that as Jews they are not already free, thinking that Jesus is referring to political freedom. John's conception of freedom should be compared to Paul's liberty of the Christian man in Romans 8:1-4, 21 and Galatians 4:21—5:1. In verses 39-41 Jesus enjoins them to do as Abraham did, for a true son must do as his father does. The reference here is possibly to the faith of Abraham, or more likely to Abraham's receiving the angels as true mesengers of God in Genesis 18:2. If you really did what he did, Jesus says, you would receive me as a true messenger of God. In verse 41 they compare their unexceptionable paternity to Jesus' paternity, and Jesus levels his final and crushing accusation: your true father is the devil, for it is his action you are really imitating, and that is the action of unbelief (verses 43-44).

The argument over Abraham continues in 8:48-59. The Jewish accusation that Jesus is a Samaritan is related to their hint in verse 41 that his parentage is irregular. The Samaritans were originally products of illegitimate unions between Gentile immigrants and Jewish women. In verses 52-53, they misunderstand his reference to eternal life, thinking he means that it involves freedom from natural death. Jesus meets this misunderstanding by openly describing his superiority to Abraham: he points to his resurrection as a gift of God (verse 54), to his knowledge of God (55), to Abraham's witness to him (56), and to his priority to Abraham (58). The "not yet fifty" in verse 57 should be taken generally, not literally. Literally, it cannot be reconciled with all our other evidence about Jesus' age. The point is the contrast between the great interval from Abraham's time to that of Jesus, and the age of Jesus himself.

5. Christ as the triumph of light, 9:1—10:42

a. the healing of the man born blind, 9:1-41

Jesus is Messiah because he is the true Son, truly witnessing to the Father. This has been the message of the previous section. Now we turn to a closely related problem: insight or sight or clarity of vision, what it means, and how it comes about.

Jesus replies to the question (John 9:3) by refusing to accept the traditional view of the relation of sin to suffering. His actual answer is difficult, but it seems to point to the man's unique value as illustrating the meaning of God's grace. In this story the real drama is the movement from unbelief to belief, not from blindness to sight, and the man must be seen primarily as a sinner moving to faith. Jesus makes clay compounded of dust and spit, anoints the eyes, and invites the man to bathe in a near-by pool which is named "the one who was sent," thus symbolically identified with Jesus himself. The bathing accomplishes the cure. It is interesting to notice the four stages in the man's apprehension of Jesus:

1. In verse 12 he doesn't even know where Jesus is. In verse 16 we see that not all the Jews acquiesce in the accusation of Jesus as sinner.

2. In verse 17, after being questioned by the Jews about the Sabbath violation on Jesus' part, he defines Jesus as a prophet because of his act of healing.

3. In verse 30, the man himself moves to a deeper level of insight; he at least knows Jesus' origin; he is from God, for he has performed the unique act of curing a man born blind. For this confession the man is excommunicated from the synagogue (9:34).

4. The final stage of insight follows Jesus' questioning of the man. Here Jesus is confessed as not merely a prophet from God, not merely a performer of unique miracles, but, as the Lord, one to be worshiped (9:38). The man's faith is contrasted to the unbelief of the Jews in verses 39-41. Jesus' answer in verse 41 means: "If you were unable to see or to believe, you would not be responsible for your unbelief; but since you are able to see or believe if you choose, you are guilty of unbelief."

b. the shepherd and the sheep, 10:1-21

1. the parable, verses 1-6

This chapter is a comment on rather than an extension of Chapter 9, and it begins with a simple parable that defines the setting for the two main affirmations that follow: that Jesus is the door to the sheepfold (in verses 7, 9) and that he is the shepherd (11, 14). The picture is that of a courtyard of a house, surrounded by a wall through which is but a single entrance. The sheep are kept in the courtyard at night; the gatekeeper will allow only the shepherd in at the gate; thieves and robbers must climb over the wall to steal the sheep.

2. interpretation of the parable, verses 10:7-21

This parable is interesting because it receives a twofold interpretation. First, Jesus is the door to the sheep. He is the way (see 14:6), the only way to life, just as the one door through the wall is the only way the sheep have of entering the courtyard. "All" in verse 8 does not refer to the Old Testament prophets, but probably to the Jews of Jesus' day and the day of the gospel's writing. But second, Jesus is the shepherd himself, for the way of life is through a continuing relationship to Jesus as God's Son.

The figure of the shepherd is a familiar one in the Old Testament (Psalm 23), and it is used in the other gospels as well (Mark 6:34 and Matthew 9:36; Matthew 18:12-14 and Luke 15:3-7). Here it receives its profoundest interpretation: the true shepherd voluntarily gives his life for his sheep (verse 11). Thieves and robbers threaten the disciples and the church from the outside; hirelings like Judas flee from within when danger comes.

Observe John 10:14-15 carefully. The disciples' security is not that they know Jesus or that Jesus knows them, but that Jesus knows the Father, the Father him, and that he gives his life for the sheep.

The parable closes with the idea of the shepherd and the sheep receding into the background. This image must give way to the deeper truth that Jesus is the true door and the true shepherd because of his death and resurrection. Verses 19-21 reveal the Jews again divided; some say he is possessed, others that he cannot be possessed because of his acts of healing.

c. conclusion, 10:22-42

The Feast of Dedication, today called Hanukkah, celebrated on December 25 the restoration of the Jewish temple by Judas Maccabaeus in 165 B.C. The Jews ask for a plain nonparabolic witness from Jesus, but he refuses, partly because his conception of the messiahship cannot be made to fit the Jewish expectation, and partly because their unbelief is perceived to flow not from inadequate evidence but from the will not to believe (10:26). In verses 27-30 Jesus again points to the basis of the security of the elect who have chosen him, and once again defines his messiahship in terms of Sonship: "I and the Father are one" (30).

This clear blasphemy (from the Jews' point of view) leads again to an attempt to take his life. Jesus appeals to his works of healing, but the Jews rightly insist that this is not the cause of offense, but rather his claim to identity with the Father. Jesus cites a passage in the Old Testament where a sort of divine status is ascribed to men, justifying himself on evidence that they are obliged to take seriously. Look at the acts of healing, Jesus adds in 37-38: are these the works of a blasphemer? Even if you cannot believe me when I speak of the Father, you must take the acts seriously. But their anger is not appeased, so Jesus goes to a place of safety from which he will finally move back to Jerusalem for the events of the last week. He goes to where John the Baptist first baptized (1:28), and the unbelief of the Jews is deliberately contrasted with John's first witness to Jesus (1:8, 29).

6. life and death, 11:1-57

Life and light have been general descriptions of the meaning of Christ, but John is not satisfied with general, nonhistorical description. In Chapter 9 he has given a specific description of Jesus as light; Chapter 11 is the specific description of Jesus as resurrection and life. In part, the chapter can be taken as an extended comment on 5:21; in part it finds its true meaning in 11:25—that the resurrection and life are not mere events of future expectation, but are beginning in the present. Finally, the story is designed as a climax to Jesus' whole controversy with the Jews, and to serve as the event which sets his arrest and crucifixion into motion (11:53).

There are synoptic events that slightly resemble this story of Lazarus: Mark 5:35-43, Luke 7:11-17. But these are isolated from their contexts in a way this story is not. And they are stories of resurrections that took place immediately after the death. Here there is an interval of four days between the death and the resurrection. It is not possible to give the reader any definite guidance on what actually took place in this event. We can, of course, decide on principle that this did not happen, merely because this kind of thing cannot happen. But perhaps it should not be quite so easy for us to make our peace with these difficult portions of the New Testament. If God is really doing something in Jesus Christ that is unique, can we decide on the impossibility of incomprehensible or improbable events with assurance?

We must, of course, take seriously the rules of probability that we inherit as modern men and women. But we must try also to give full weight to the implications of such faith in God as we happen to hold. Recognizing this inevitable and permanent tension, it is better not to go through this gospel wondering about the factual historicity of each event as it comes, but rather to devote ourselves to the task of understanding what the author is trying to do and say as he shapes his material and presents his witness. So, if it is difficult to say what actually happened, it is easy to say what is meant by the story: the new life coming from God in Jesus' person and work is powerfully present now. It is not merely a hope, it is a present fact; and it is a fact that is far greater than anything we deserve or expect.

John assumes the reader's familiarity with the household of Mary and Martha at Bethany, as recorded in Luke 10:38-42 and in Mark 14:3-9. The actual events as recorded are not particularly elusive.

Jesus' response to the sisters in John 11:4 is ambiguous: he means that Lazarus' death will be temporary; his hearers seem to interpret him to mean that the illness is not serious. Two meanings also may be found in Jesus' statement that the Son of God will be glorified by means of the illness (11:4): his power will be manifest through it, and the raising will actually lead to the arrest, death, and resurrection, which will finally validate his glorification.

Martha comes to meet Jesus and mildly reproaches him for his delay (11:21). Jesus' reply in verse 23 is taken by Martha as a word of pious consolation, but Jesus sharply defines his meaning: the power of the resurrection life is not something to be waited for in the future; it is now present. Martha responds in verse 27 with a far deeper confession of faith than she had offered in verse 22.

Verses 33-38 offer us a deeply moving portrayal of Jesus' grief, though verse 33 suggests anger as well as grief in the original Greek. The grief may be taken as a mark of his true humanity, as a kind of agony in the presence of death (like the synoptic accounts of Jesus' Gethsemane prayer). Or we may say that the real source of the grief and anger is the unbelief of the Jews (11:37) and the half-belief of Martha (11:39).

The miracle itself is described vividly and simply, verse 44 being in some ways the most striking and the most incredible touch of all. (The reader may want to refer to the parable in Luke 16:19-31 in which a reference is made to the hypothetical resurrection of Lazarus. Some have thought that John's story is a development in narrative form of this parable.)

The miracle, as usual, causes a division among the Jews, who meet to decide on some action. In John 11:49-50 the high priest, Caiaphas, decides to move against Jesus. His decision is in fact a shrewdly calculated political move to avoid Roman intervention. But John interprets his saying in verse 50 as a curious kind of prediction of the universal significance of Jesus' death (11:51-52).

Jesus withdraws, the Passover draws near, the Jews in the temple prepare to arrest Jesus should he come to Jerusalem. Verse 57 is doubtless added to explain the cause of Judas' betrayal that may have been confusing in the earlier synoptic tradition.

7. life through death, 12:1-36, and the author's summary of the material in 2:1—12:36, 12:37-50

The story of the anointing has a similarity both to Mark 14:3-9 and to Luke 7:36-50. John seems to have combined both these pieces of material. Judas is identified as the one who complains about the waste of money. John 12:7-8 means that although the poor are always to be served, Mary's humble act is a worthy one and cannot be criticized as wasteful; for, in anointing Jesus, she does two things: she declares him to be the anointed one or Messiah, and she points forward to his death, since the dead are prepared for burial with costly ointments.

John's treatment of the entry into the city is also closely related to the synoptic versions. The crowds seem to greet Jesus as a political or royal Messiah, but apparently (12:16) the disciples do not betray any understanding of what is going on. Verses 17-18 mention that the crowd's enthusiasm is based on Jesus' miraculous act of raising Lazarus.

The world has gone after him, the Pharisees complain in John 12:19; and verse 20 gives an example: the Greeks seek out Jesus. The Greeks are always on the edge of the gospel, for they do not really "come to" Jesus until the resurrection; but the Jews are passing from the center of the picture now; from Chapter 13 on, everything concerns Jesus and the disciples. Jesus' words in response to the Greeks' request (verses 23-26) are familiar descriptions of the meaning of obedience and discipleship.

However, (in 12:27-36) the obedience of the disciple is based on the radical obedience of the Son. Verses 27-30 reflect the agony at Gethsemane, reminding us that Jesus' obedience is unto death. The Jews object that they have never heard anything about a suffering Messiah; Jesus affirms himself to be the suffering Son of man and Messiah, and invites them once more to choose. Note the tension between the apparent inevitability of Jewish unbelief (12:39) and the affirmation that some did in fact believe (12:42). John's predestinarian views are never consistent.

John 12:44-50 sums up the message of the whole gospel up to this point: obedience, the meaning of Christ, judgment, and eternal life. The obedience means suffering and death.

III. The Passion of Jesus Christ

13:1—21:35

1. the farewell discourses, 13:1—17:26

These chapters contain discourses given by Jesus to his disciples that prepare them for what is to follow. For Christians they are John's profound interpretation of this central event for the life of the church in any day.

a. the footwashing and its meaning, 13:1-30

John 13:1-3 gives the theological context for the story. The time has come for the disciples to be prepared. The synoptic gospels record at this point the Lord's Supper; John has chosen another way to make his point. There are reflections both of baptism and of the Lord's Supper here, but we are likely to recall primarily the description of Jesus in the other gospels as servant of all (Luke 22:27, for example). But this is not merely an example of humility (girding with a towel is the action of a slave, 13:4); the deeper point is that the disciple's real cleansing from sin will be consummated in an even greater act of humility than this one—in the death of Christ itself. "To the end" (13:1) thus means "to the end of his life, unto death."

John 13:12-17 interprets the act of foot-washing. The disciples must show the same humility to all men that Jesus has just displayed to them. In verses 21-30, the betrayal is predicted. Jesus is portrayed here with a special kind of foresight into Judas' treachery, and the only "explanation" of that treachery is that Satan entered into him. The "beloved disciple"—presumably John—is explicitly mentioned in verse 23, and he alone is told the identity of the betrayer. Verse 23 also reminds us that the disciples do not sit at table, but recline on couches, generally resting on the left elbow; John, on Jesus' right, would thus be described as "close to the breast of Jesus" (13:25).

b. the first discourse: Christ's departure and the security of the disciples, 13:31—14:31

This section, apparently concluding with the dismissal of the disciples from the upper room (14:31) is sometimes called the first discourse. But there is some evidence that 13:31—14:31 is a version of the same discourse that we have in longer form in Chapters 15-17. The structure and many of the themes are repeated in the second and longer passage. This is the most adequate explanation for the otherwise puzzling words at the end of 14:31 which seem to indicate a full break.

With 13:31 the hour of glorification has now fully arrived. It had partly been coming up to now (2:4, 7:30, 8:20, and see also 17:1) but the last hour is decisively present and the disciples can now receive it fully. However, it will mean Jesus' separation from his disciples, a separation that the disciples cannot now overcome. Why? Because the "hour" for their death has not yet arrived. Their function now is not to die, but to love one another. In this "not yet" interval between Jesus' death and their own, the love commandment must be put to work. To love one another is not a narrowing of the universal love of neighbor found in the Sermon on the Mount. It is a mutual love in the church that has as its purpose the salvation of all. What we do not find here is the command to love the neighbor "as thyself" (Matthew 19:19, 22:39).

Peter (verses 36-38) does not entirely understand this departure of Jesus, just as he partly misunderstood the footwashing (13:8). He is still too proud to follow Jesus in his humility, but verse 37 suggests that Peter's way may ultimately involve martyrdom, as 21:18-19 clearly states. His denial is predicted.

Chapter 14 is a word of consolation to the disciples facing the loss of their Lord; their security must be firmly based so that they can face the coming events without fear or despair, and so that they can serve the Lord in his absence.

Their security rests on Christ, and on his preparing a place for them with God. "I will come again" in John 14:3 may mean the disciples' death, and it may mean the new union with Christ in the resurrection and gift of the Spirit. This point on the goal of human life is so important that John moves into a dialogue form to clarify it. Thomas tells Jesus that he does not know either the way or the goal; and the answer is that the way is Jesus in his humility and death, and that God is the goal. Philip wants a miracle to render this goal as clear as possible (verse 8) and he is told that he has already had all the miracle he is ever going to get, Jesus Christ himself.

With John 14:12 we are reminded that belief or faith in Christ involves both works and prayer. The greater works of the disciples (verse 12) may refer to the conversion of the Gentiles and the expansion of the church in the world. These greater works of love require Jesus' departure before they can begin, but God's presence will be with them, now in a different form from that of the historical Christ: the Counselor, the Spirit of Truth. Verses 15-17 are the first of the sayings on this subject, which we also find in John 14:25-26, 15:26; 16:5-11, and 16:13-15.

There is no explicit doctrine of the Trinity in the gospels, but these sayings about the Counselor became important material for the formation of that doctrine when, because of certain external pressures in the fourth century, the relation between God, Jesus Christ, and the Holy Spirit needed to be made explicit. The early Christians found that God was present with them in a special way after the death and resurrection, but in a way that was closely dependent on Jesus' actual life and ministry. They came to formulate this unique presence in terms of the doctrine of the Holy Spirit, and these sayings about the Counselor bear directly on that later formulation. The church became Trinitarian not because of some speculative interest in the number three, but because certain events had happened in their midst which they could interpret only by saying that Father, Son, and Spirit, though one God, are somehow three distinguishable forms of his presence.

But the final and deepest assurance of all is the resurrection of Christ. This is the meaning of John 14:18; it does not refer to a future second coming. Through the resurrection the mutual involvement of Father, Son, and disciples will be consummated, but this involvement still requires the obligation of love.

Thus the disciples are prepared to face the coming tragedy with the security and peace (14:27) that only Christ can give them. It is not the absence of conflict, which the world calls peace, but the peace of confidence in God's rule and his promise of life to those who believe in him.

c. the second discourse, Christ and his church, 15:1—16:33

1. the relation of the Christian to the risen Lord, 15:1-17

In 6:56 the relation between the disciple and Christ was described as eating his flesh and drinking his blood. Chapter 6 itself dealt with Jesus as living bread; here we come (in the upper room, notice) to the second half of the Lord's Supper symbolism: Jesus as the true vine.

Vineyard imagery is familiar in both the Old and the New Testament; see Mark 12:1-9. There the vineyard was Israel; its rejection of Christ and its unfruitfulness was the point. Here the vine is Christ himself, and the context is not the rejection of Christ by the Jews (John has already dealt with this extensively) but the life of the church and the presence of Christ in the church to the true believer.

Here the true believer is simply defined as one in union with Christ. The details of the allegory are not difficult to apply. From this union a number of consequences flow: in Christ, the believer serves Christ (bears fruit, John 15:2, 4, 16), finds his prayer answered (verses 7, 16; compare 14:13-14), knows the meaning of obedient love (verses 9-13, 17), and has his very life (verse 6) and true joy (11). All this is not an achievement of the believer, it is the gift of Christ himself (16).

Verse 6 is unlike John's usual idea of judgment, and reminds us of the older emphasis in Matthew 5:13.

2. *the Christian and the hostile world, 15:18—16:15*

15:18-25 relates the world's hatred of the Christians, as shown in the persecutions of John's own day, to the hatred of Christ that led to the crucifixion. The love of the disciples is in sharpest contrast to the hatred of the world. Hatred from the world is to be expected; when it is a hatred and a rejection that proceeds from a knowledge of Christ it is morally culpable and sinful (verse 22). Indeed, the world's knowing rejection of Christ and his disciples is hatred of God himself.

Verses 26-27 introduce another saying about the Counselor, who will bear witness with the disciples in the midst of their struggle with the hostile world.

In 16:1-4 the hostility of the Jews is made even more definite: it will involve excommunication from the synagogue and even death for the disciples. But even so (verses 5-11 continue in another saying about the Counselor), joy and not sorrow should be the response of the disciples. The Counselor is the new form of the presence of Christ in the Church; so it is essential that Christ himself depart to the Father. The work of the Counselor must involve a stern judgment of the world.

The final Counselor saying in verses 13-15 really sums up the content of the preaching of the church; it is to be a proclamation utterly dependent on God, and it will declare the true meaning of the new age, ushered in completely by the death and resurrection. (This is the meaning of "the things that are to come" in verse 13; it does not refer to the ability to foretell the future.) The Counselor, here called the Spirit of truth, is the very presence of Christ in the midst of his people, bringing to them the riches of God himself and empowering them to claim it and to declare it to all.

3. the disciples and the death and resurrection of Christ, 16:16-33

The "going" is probably the death of Christ and the "coming," the resurrection, with "the little while" the interval between, though this may be deliberately ambiguous, so that the interval between the ascension and the second coming may also be suggested. Verse 20 describes the joy of the world over Christ's death that will turn into the sorrow of judgment, and compares this with the disciples' sorrow that will turn to joy. Verse 22 again refers to the resurrection; after this climax there will be no more anxious questions to Jesus, but only faithful prayer to God.

In verses 29-33 the disciples think they see it all. They suspect that Jesus' going to the Father can be consummated without his death, and they decide that he did indeed come from God because of his omniscience. Jesus rudely shatters their self-confidence and predicts their flight after the crucifixion. But, in the final verse which can be taken as a summary of the whole second discourse, even their despair is seen as a temporary tribulation that will be put aside because of Jesus' victory over the world. Note that "tribulations" are not overcome; these still come to every disciple. But Jesus' victory makes it possible for the disciple to meet every tribulation with faith in Christ as God's Son.

d. the prayer of Christ, 17:1-26

In this final prayer, the meaning of "the hour" of glorification is revealed. The teaching is completed; the truth has been given the disciples, and they will receive it fully through the power of the Spirit after the resurrection. One thing remains to be done: Christ consecrates himself in the presence of the disciples (17:19). He prays first for himself (verses 1-5), then for the disciples and their future in the church (6-18), and finally for the whole church in time and in eternity (20-26). Nearly all the themes of the Johannine theology are contained here: obedience unto death as the meaning of God's glory in Christ; the disciples' being in, but not of, the world; the revelation to the disciples of the true character ("name," verse 6) of God in Christ; their mission, their unity in love, and their present and future relation to God and to Christ.

In 17:1-5 we discover that the chief result of the Father's glorification of the Son, and the Son's of the Father, is the gift of eternal life to the disciples here and now. This life is defined clearly as the knowledge of God who sent Jesus into the world.

In 17:6-18 Jesus describes what he has done for the disciples. Note that his chief work is not teaching or healing but the calling of a distinctive community to bear witness to God by making known His "name." He asks God that the disciples be kept faithful, in but not of the world, bearing witness to what they know, united to each other as Son is united to the Father. The reference in verse 12 is, of course, to Judas; and in verse 14 John is apparently thinking of the world's hatred in terms of the persecutions in the midst of which he is living. In verse 17 Jesus prays for the sanctification of the disciples: that they be dedicated and empowered to bear witness to the truth. This dedication is not based on anything they have of themselves; it is based on Jesus' own consecration. "Consecrate" in verse 19, the climax of the prayer, is a sacrificial term; it refers directly to his death, and it means "I dedicate myself as a sacrificial offering."

Finally, in John 17:20-26, Jesus prays for the church present and to come. This is a prayer for the church's unity, based on the unity of Son with Father, that the church may be so bound to God and to Christ that the world will believe its witness. In verse 24 we pass from present to future, and we catch a glimpse of the eschatological hope of the church. The three stages of Christian existence are thus sketched out: first is the time of the manifestation of God's glory through Christ to the disciples; second is the new form of presence of Christ in the church after his death and resurrection (this is where John was, and where we are now); finally, there is the consummation of the church in the perfect love of the presence of God.

2. the narrative of the Passion and resurrection, 18:1—21:25

a. the Passion, 18:1—19:42

1. the arrest, 18:1-11

The scene suggests Gethsemane; note "garden" in John 18:1 and the reference to the cup of suffering in verse 11. There are some new features that we do not find in the synoptic accounts; no kiss from Judas; the identification of Peter as the one who cuts off the slave's ear; the emphasis on Jesus' moral authority and courage in verse 6; and Jesus' concern for the safety of the other disciples in verse 8. The main impression we receive from this account is that Jesus, and not Judas or the soldiers, is in control. The arrest, the suffering, the death must come, for it is all God's will and the means He uses to glorify Himself through the Son. But it would be wrong to conclude from this that all death and suffering can be fully described as being simply God's will. This particular suffering and death is just that, for it is the center of God's gift of salvation to sinful men. But human suffering and death are often due to human evil, to disease, to accident; and suffering is an enemy that must be fought and, whenever possible, removed. God's will is present to us in every suffering, but it is too easy to explain suffering away by saying only that it is God's will.

2. *the trial before the high priest and Peter's denial, 18:12-27*

There is some difficulty about Annas and Caiaphas here. It is the latter who is high priest (see Matthew 26:57 and John 11:49), yet Jesus is taken to Annas, and there is only a hint of a trial before Caiaphas in verse 24. The other disciple in verse 15 is probably the beloved disciple.

The strange thing about the trial before Annas is its brevity, compared to Pilate's extended examination. Jesus is questioned only about his disciples and his teaching. There are no messianic questions, no mention of this threat to destroy the temple. No accusations are made and no charge is established or even defined. Jesus refuses to testify against himself (18:21) which is in fact illegal in any case: evidence must come from witnesses, not from the accused. So the examination is inadequate, illegal, and, in verse 22, brutal.

3. *the trial before Pilate, 18:28—19:16*

Jesus is taken into Pilate's residence, the praetorium; the Jews remain outside for fear of ritual defilement. The discussion that follows between Jesus and Pilate takes place inside, and Pilate goes outside to consult with the Jews when necessary. If the Jews here represent those who reject Christ, Pilate stands for the world that needs a Christ, half-convinced, half-skeptical.

Pilate returns to Jesus (18:33) and asks him if he is the Messiah. We may well wonder where Pilate picked up this accusation, and indeed we perhaps ought to be somewhat skeptical of the historical accuracy of these private conversations between Pilate and Jesus. It is hard to see how they could have come to be known. Jesus penetrates to the heart of the theological issue and discusses the nature of kingship, affirming his true kingship, denying that he is a king in Pilate's sense. Verses 33-38 are really a study of the relation of the church and the empire, and their relevance to John's own day can easily be seen.

After the half-ironic, half-sincere question "What is truth?", Pilate again tries to avoid action by citing to the Jews the custom of releasing a prisoner on the Passover. The Jews refuse to accept Jesus' release.

Verses 1-6 are difficult to understand. Perhaps Pilate is trying to appeal to the pity of the Jews. He whips Jesus, making him appear so powerless that they would conclude he could not be dangerous. Pilate's scornful "Here is the man!" in verse 5 is an indirect witness to the truth; here *is* the man indeed, the very word made flesh, the Son of man himself.

But Jewish sympathy cannot be aroused, and they make their second accusation: he has made himself the Son of God. Here the Jews blurt out their real charge against Jesus, though up to now they had doubtless been afraid to admit to Pilate that their objections were religious and not political. This accusation upsets Pilate, and he questions Jesus again, in verses 9-11. Jesus answers with a discussion of the nature of authority.

Again Pilate tries to free Jesus, and the Jews openly threaten Pilate with being friendly with an enemy of the imperial authority. The final charge they bring is rebellion, and to make their accusation convincing they utter a word of blasphemy and final apostasy: "We have no king but Caesar" (19:15). Pilate finally gives in, and consents to have him crucified. Verse 16 does not mean that the Jews crucified him. Verses 17, 18, and 23 remind us that the soldiers of Rome were the actual agents of the execution. Pilate's actual responsibility remains: for John the Son of man must be "lifted up," crucified, so the Roman means of punishment is essential. But the author certainly minimizes Pilate's actual involvement.

4. crucifixion and burial, 19:17-42

The details of the crucifixion are more carefully related to fulfillment of scripture here than in the synoptics, and the symbolic meaning of these details is brought to the fore. The story of the seamless robe, verses 23-24, becomes a parable of the unity of the church.

Mark 15:40 and Matthew 27:56 mention these women near the cross, but there the third is Salome and not Mary the wife of Clopas. This is the first mention of Mary Magdalene in the gospel, and she comes in later as a witness of the resurrection. She is also a witness of the resurrection in the other gospels, and Luke 8:2 briefly mentions her. This is all the real information we have of her. There is no good evidence to identify her with Mary of Bethany in Mark 14:3-9 or with the sinner in Luke 7:37.

John reports three sayings from the cross; in the first, Jesus gives the care of his mother to the beloved disciple. It is hard to see any important symbolic or theological meaning for this; perhaps it is merely a touch describing the church as a new kind of family. "I thirst" is a fulfillment of Psalm 69:21. Hyssop is an herb. A twig of hyssop may be meant here, and this would relate the death again to the Passover, for hyssop is used in some of the Passover ceremonies. But it is hard to see how a sponge could be placed on a small branch and offered to Jesus. The Greek word for soldier's spear or javelin is very similar to the Greek word for hyssop, and there may be a scribe's error here. Putting the sponge on a javelin would be more intelligible in this context.

The breaking of the other criminal's legs is a detail peculiar to John, as is the reference to the Old Testament to explain why Jesus' legs were not broken. The point of John 19:31-37 is mainly to insist on the reality of Jesus' death (verse 33) on the day before Passover, to emphasize that his death coincided with the killing of the Passover lambs. He really died, in accord with God's will and the scripture. Verses 34-35 state that this death gives life and cleansing for all (the witness is again the beloved disciple).

John does add symbolic and interpretative touches to some of the incidents of the crucifixion. But at the same time he insists on the real historic character of the central event. Jesus Christ, the Son of God, really died and was really buried.

b. the resurrection, 20:1—21:25

1. the empty tomb, 20:1-29

There are two parts to this account, verses 1-18 concerned with Mary, 19-29 with Thomas. The vivid details are not difficult to grasp. The beloved disciple, hearing the report of the women, reaches the tomb first, but Peter goes in first. The description of the linen cloths that he sees (verses 6-7) suggests that the body was not disturbed or stolen, but that it dematerialized in some miraculous way. However, it is not Peter but the beloved disciple who is the first to believe. The faith of the beloved disciple who believed without seeing the risen Lord is the center of this part of the story. Mary sees the empty tomb but continues to weep. She does not believe until the one she takes for the gardener speaks to her and she responds to the risen Lord. This account is an interesting study of the relation of sight (facts) to faith. Mary, the beloved disciple, and, in the next section, Thomas—each has the problem of facts and faith solved in a slightly different way.

Later that evening, John 20:19-25, Jesus appears to a group of disciples, shows them the marks of his victory over the world, and gives them their final commission to serve. John records the gift of the Spirit, the power to undertake the commission, as occurring on Easter Sunday rather than on Pentecost, six weeks later, as in Acts

2. Verse 23 defines the chief purpose of the church as forgiveness of sins and the withholding of forgiveness or judgment.

Thomas, whom we have met before as something of a pessimist and skeptic (11:16 and 14:5), hears the report of Jesus' appearance, and remains unconvinced. The next week Jesus comes to Thomas, who responds, not merely identifying the figure with Jesus, but affirming him as Lord and as God. In verse 29, Jesus mildly rebukes Thomas, or at least praises those who believe without seeing.

This chapter is very carefully written. Mary's tears and Thomas' doubts are parallel; in both parts, the problem of touching Jesus is raised; in the first part, Mary's tears are less important than the faith of the beloved disciple; in the second, Thomas' doubt is less important than the commission of the disciples.

Verses 30-31 conclude with a comment on the gospel John has written, and with a final word on its function. Many have felt that this marked the true ending of the gospel at one time, and that Chapter 21 represents a later addition, perhaps by the same hand as Chapters 1-20. To some, Chapter 21 seems anticlimactic; to others, the further explanation of the mission of the disciples and the comments on the faith of Peter and the beloved disciple are quite appropriate.

2. *epilogue, 21:1-25*

a. the appearance by the lake, 21:1-14

This story reminds us a little of Luke 5:1-11, but it would be a mistake to read it simply as a story of a wonderful catch of fish. There are a number of touches that suggest a deeper meaning playing throughout the story, even if it is difficult to know just how far we should take the symbolism. The language reminiscent of the Lord's Supper in John 21:13 is clear; the untorn net of verse 11 may suggest the capacity of the church to hold all sorts of men. The number 153 has been a happy hunting ground for symbolic interpreters. Two points should be noted, which may or may not be relevant: 153 is the sum of the first 17 whole numbers, and 17 is the sum of 7 and 10—both supposed to be numbers symbolizing wholeness or perfection. It used to be thought that ancient Greek zoologists had estimated the number of types of fish to be 153, so that the number was said to symbolize a perfect and a complete catch.

b. Peter and the beloved disciple, 21:15-23

If the catch of fish represents the mission to the unconverted, the words to Peter perhaps represent the mission to the converted, to the sheep. Peter's threefold response of love is intended to suggest his threefold denial, and to indicate that it is overcome. Peter's death is hinted at in John 21:18-19; though verse 18 seems more like a prediction and 19 more like the statement of a fact already accomplished. Notice that Jesus' last word to Peter (verse 19) is the same as his first, in Mark 1:17—"Follow me."

Verses 20-23 are a slight rebuke to Peter for being concerned about the fact that the beloved disciple is to have a longer period of service than Peter himself. The chapter ends with a statement on the trustworthiness of the witness of the beloved disciple, and a remark, like that in 20:30-31, about the many things which the gospel has excluded. The "I" of "I suppose" in verse 25 is the author; but whether this is the beloved disciple or not we have no means of knowing. The author deliberately kept himself out of his gospel except for this brief allusion; his function was to witness to something far more significant than himself.